PET LIBRARY'S

# Parakeet

## Guide

PET LIBRARY'S

# Parakeet
# Guide

## by Cyril Rogers

### England

THE PET LIBRARY LTD

The Pet Library Ltd.,
Subsidiary of Sternco In-
dustries Inc., 600 South
Fourth Street, Harrison,
N.J. Exclusive Canadian
Distributor: Hartz Moun-
tain Pet Supplies Limited,
1125 Talbot Street, St.
Thomas, Ontario, Canada.
Exclusive United King-
dom Distributor: The Pet
Library (London) Ltd.,
30 Borough High Street,
London S.E. 1.

© 1970 Cyril Rogers
(England)

Printed in the Netherlands

ISBN 0-87826-856-1

# Table of Contents

Photos of single parakeets for type and color: Horst Müller.

Cover photo: Harry Lacey

The budgerigar is the most widely loved of all pet birds.

# Introduction

This book is an "armchair guide" to the world of budgerigars —parakeets to my American readers—an important part of the fascinating world of parrots, of which there are over 300 species.

It is an introduction to the keeping of budgerigars as pets, and their breeding in control aviaries, but a detailed discussion of the various color mutations and their genetic makeup has not been overlooked.

Since this book is being directed to all English speaking peoples I use the names *budgerigar, budgie, parakeet* and *keet* interchangeably. The correct American name for the species is Australian Shell Parakeet, a name that refers to the bird's distinctive marking: a zebra-striped or seashell pattern of black across its head, neck and wings, but this is usually shortened to just "Parakeet."

The budgerigar, most widely loved of all pet birds—it has now surpassed the canary in popularity—has journeyed from its place of origin in Australia to every country in the world, and the millions now living in captivity, which certainly exceed those living in the original wild state, are proof of their successful domestication.

From its original color of grass green it has been bred in a host of new colors, patterns and combinations of color—all the colors of the rainbow except red, and even this may have appeared by the time this book sees the light of print.

Undoubtedly the genetic possibilities in breeding these different color mutations—theoretically there are hundreds of combinations possible—have helped to increase the budgerigars' popularity with geneticists, but their great appeal to the general public has been, and always will be, their pert gaiety and ability to mimic the human voice.

Budgies can be happy in the smallest apartment, and can

Budgies can live in almost any cage.

HORST MÜLLER

live in almost any cage. They are inexpensive to purchase and maintain, and if cared for properly, extremely hardy. Their life-span is about seven years. They are clean birds, although like most seedeaters they do scatter dry hulls. Their droppings are small and firm, and can easily be picked up with tissue; this is why most housekeepers are perfectly willing to let them fly about the house and ride around on their shoulders.

Budgies have therapeutic value; they are kept in mental hospitals and convalescent homes to give patients a new interest in life. The entire mating, nesting and rearing of the young is an extremely interesting procedure to watch. They make extremely happy pets for shut-ins and elderly people. It is surprising how quickly a budgie becomes attached to a person confined to bed. This is probably because the invalid has more than the average amount of time to devote to his pet.

The budgie has an educational value. Schools include budgerigar breeding in their biology classes to demonstrate reproduction and the laws of genetics. Budgies are ideal for this purpose because the results of cross pairings can be seen clearly in the colors of their young. Birds used in science projects usually become extremely tame and carry out their domestic duties as the students watch, from laying their eggs and incubating them to rearing and feeding their young.

If you already have your budgie this book should, of course, prove invaluable, but if you have not yet made your selection, it will be even more so. Since choosing the right budgie is the most important step of all, I will sum up the basics briefly and then go into greater detail further along in the book. First of all, pick the youngest and healthiest bird possible. Whether or not a budgie learns to talk depends entirely on the patient training you give him, and the age at which you begin. There does not seem to be such a thing as a "talking strain" of budgerigars. Also, it is difficult to deter-mine the sex of a baby budgerigar. When the birds are older their ceres (wattles), the waxlike area surrounding their nostrils, will show the difference (bright blue for males, light blue, buff or brown for females), but in the baby birds all ceres are the same color, and only highly experienced breeders can sex them at an early age.

HARRY LACEY

Whether or not a budgie learns to talk depends entirely on the patient training you give him, and his age when you begin.

This highly bred Blue show cock is a far cry from the original wild budgerigar. It is larger, more robust and more colorful.

Societies have been organized to promote the breeding and displaying of the many color varieties that have been evolved by controlled breeding. The two leading ones in the USA are:

> The American Budgerigar Society
> 4424 Cane Run Road,
> Louisville, Kentucky 40216

> The United Budgerigar Society
> 71 Chimney Lane
> Levittown, Long Island, New York 11756

In Great Britain, it is:

> The Budgerigar Society
> Bank Chambers, 6 Grove Lane
> Birmingham 21, England

# Budgerigars at a Glance

Common name: Budgerigar, Shell Parakeet
Scientific name: *Melopsittacus undulatus*
Diet: Seeds, grain, fruits, vegetables
Water: Drinks little, but should have access to an un-
limited quantity
Best age to purchase: 6 weeks
Life-span: 7 years; some live 20
First molt: About 3 months
Molting season: Usually spring, but can be any time
Mating time: Any time; usually spring
Mating habit: Will pair for life, but will philander if
given the opportunity
Nest: In wild, in tree hollows; in captivity, in wooden
or cardboard nest boxes
Number of eggs: 3 to 10, average 5; (only 4 should be
raised by the parents)
Incubation period: Eggs take 18 days to hatch
How to tell a young one: The head and brow are
striped; the eyes solid black; the cere tannish pink
Colors: Green, Blue, Yellow, White, Violet
Sex distinction: In general, cere of males bright blue,
that of females light blue, flesh, buff, brown
Training age: 5 to 8 weeks
Talking ability: Both sexes
Best number to keep: Any number may be kept
together; for talking and training one is best
Age at leaving nest: 5 weeks

# I   History

Soon after the continent of Australia, discovered by Captain James Cook in 1770, was explored, small green birds, in flocks at times so great that they seemed to darken the sky, were observed. These tiny parrots were described in various learned papers with a few vague particulars and descriptions.

The earliest mention was by a naturalist named George Shaw in "Zoology of New Holland" about 1793, and the first known drawing of the species appeared in "Naturalists' Miscellany" in 1805.

Since their discovery, the birds have been known by many different names; their earliest name, "Undulated Parakeet," was bestowed on them by Shaw, but since then their popularity has resulted in a plethora of names, Zebra Parakeet, Warbling Grass Parakeet, Shell Parakeet or Parrot, Waved Parrot and Canary Parrot being the most popular. Until fairly recently they were also called Love Birds, but this name is now used exclusively to designate members of the genus *Agapornis*, a group of small parrots from Africa.

All these names fit this little green bird very well, but strangely enough, it was the name given them by the Australian aborigines, "Betcherrygah," that has stuck. Because this means "pretty good eating," it is apparent that the natives found them tasty morsels. The English have simply made the name more pronounceable.

Until 1840, it appears, the only budgerigars seen outside of Australia were stuffed and mounted. As late as 1837, John Gould (1804–1881), the famous English naturalist, wrote:

> *A single example of the female of this elegant little Parrot has been for many years in the collection of the Linnean Society; two other collections are referred to by Dr. Latham as containing specimens. It is only within the last few years that the male has become known. It was discovered in the greatest abundance by Captain Stuart during his journey into the interior of New South Wales; and specimens were transmitted by him to the Zoological Society, together with many other interesting birds. This gentleman informed me that on the*

*extensive plains bordering the Murrumbridgu, he met with this lovely species in immense flocks, feeding on the seeds and berries of the low stunted bushes called scrubs, so abundant in those flat countries.*

*I have also received several individuals in a collection sent to me by Mr. C. Coxen, which he had procured to the north of the Hunter's River.*

*In their habits all the members of this group are extremely quick and active, running on the ground with great facility much after the manner of the true* Platy cerci *or* Ground Parrakeets, *to which they are closely allied in affinity. The present species differs from all other members of the group in the round, drop-like markings of the cheeks and throat, in its rich green colouring in the prolonged centre tail feathers. Of its nest, eggs, etc., nothing is known.*

Three years later Gould himself introduced the first live budgerigars to England. "I was one of the first," he was to state many years later, "who introduced living examples to this country, having succeeded in bringing home several on my return in 1840." They sold for what was then about $125. These birds had been bred and raised in Australia by Gould's brother-in-law, Charles Coxen, so by then, obviously, their breeding habits had become known. Gould gave the bird its scientific name, *Melopsittacus undulatus.* Before then Shaw had classified it *Psittacus undulatus.*

In nature, as I have pointed out, budgerigars once lived in such numbers on the plains of Australia that travelers spoke of flocks that blackened the sky and filled the air with the whirr of their wings. Some flocks were so large that they were thought to be approaching dust storms. In their flight, as they spiral high, the wild green birds make a dazzling sight, and when they cluster on the limbs of a dead tree, they appear, as one observer so aptly put it, "to clothe it again in foliage."

Gould's first importation was, in the years to come, followed by innumerable others. The hundreds of thousands of budgies brought to Europe in the second half of the nineteenth century attest to their run-away popularity. One ship alone, arriving in 1868, landed 10,000 birds; one London dealer is said to have sold 15,000 pairs in four months.

Times have changed! The Australian aborigines looked on parakeets as a delicacy. Today, we share our delicacies with them.

The whole thing was getting out of hand! In 1894 the Australian government stopped the exportation of the wild birds, but by then there was no shortage; budgies were already being bred in Europe.

According to Karl Russ, the German ornithologist, the Countess Von Schwerin was the first European to breed budgies; this was in Berlin in 1855. The whole thing came as a surprise to the Countess, or so it would seem, as Russ reports it:

> The female laid the first eggs in a corner on the bottom of the cage. Not knowing the natural instinct of parrots to nest in tree holes, the lady fitted a nest, such as is used for canaries, to the top of the cage, and the eggs were put into this. Twice in succession they (the parents) carefully carried the eggs, stuck under the chin, in an undamaged condition, back to the first spot and there the female sat over her five eggs. Two young ones were successfully reared.

With the Countess leading the way, it was soon realized that budgerigars would breed in England and on the Continent. Belgium, France and Germany were among the first and Australia's ban was hardly felt at all. By the turn of the century, parakeets were being bred by the hundreds of thousands. In one establishment alone, the Bastide Aviaries in Toulouse, France, it was said, 120,000 budgies had to be destroyed when World War I began.

The war ended in 1918, and by 1920 the stock was beginning to build again, this time with the then-new blue, mauve, cobalt and white varieties.

## Color Mutations

It is not surprising that, in view of the quantities, mutations soon began to occur. Mutations, of course, appear among wild birds as well (yellows have been sighted in Australia), but because feral birds breed indiscriminately, the mutations quickly disappear, overwhelmed, so to speak, by the dominant light green of the "basic" birds.

Light yellow was the first mutation to appear; this occurred in Belgium in the 1870's. Both the black-eyed and red-eyed varieties came into being. However, since at that time the science of genetics was unknown, the red-eyed variety (which we now know to be sex-linked) disappeared. But the black-eyed yellow was fixed, and still exists. Joseph Abrahams was the first to breed light yellows in England.

Undoubtedly the biggest event in the budgerigar world was the appearance in the early 1880's of a blue budgie. This mutation—the Sky Blue—was carefully preserved, but it was not until 1910 that Sky Blues were seen in Great Britain. They were shown at the Horticultural Hall in November of that year, and at the Crystal Palace in 1911. Mr Pelham Sutton, in 1912, was the first to breed Sky Blues in England.

I can well understand the fanciers of that day being amazed at the delicate coloration of the Sky Blues, as when I saw my first examples in 1920 I found it hard to believe that such birds existed. The Duke of Bedford believed them to be unique in the bird world. He stated that their singular beauty occurs in no other living bird: ". . . the combination of snow white and sky blue which nature, without the aid of human art, only seems to provide in inanimate forms."

## The Big Boom

In the mid-twenties, there was a curious "Budgerigar Boom" that lasted for two or three years. While it started in Japan, its repercussions were felt in many other countries and par-

In addition to the color mutations, budgies with caps or crests have also been developed.

ticularly in England. The story is a romantic one, at least in its beginning. It all began when a Japanese nobleman gave a pair of Sky Blue budgies to his sweetheart as a "love token" — remember, in those days, budgies were still commonly called Love Birds, and that the blue and white was comparatively rare. Remember, too, that blue and white are favorite colors of the Japanese. Little wonder then that the giving of these delicately colored birds to one's loved one became all the rage in Japan.

There were not enough birds to supply the demand, so they had to be imported from other countries. Demand exceeded supply. Prices went sky high. The values rose to as much as $500 and more for a pair of Sky Blues, Cobalts, Whites or Mauves. According to the late Harry Humphries, one time secretary of England's Budgerigar Society, "The highest price ever obtained was for a pair of Whites. (We knew then only the one shade or suffusion—the present-day White Sky Blue.) They were sent out to a member of the Royal House of Japan, who paid a fabulous sum (reportedly

$5,000) for them—and both birds were dead on arrival."

With prices like these, everyone tried to get into the act. Persons who had never heard of budgerigars started breeding them. It was like finding diamonds in your own back yard, but like America's chinchilla boom in the fifties the whole thing got out of hand. Then in 1927 the Japanese government banned their importation—by this time Japanese breeders were turning them out in quantity—and, like the chinchilla boom, the market collapsed. Amateur and professional breeders alike were stuck. Prices tumbled overnight, and those who had sunk a great deal of money into breeding pairs were never able to recover their investments. Remember, these were not the fine exhibition or breeding specimens that we know today. They were run of the mill, pet quality adult birds. (Babies were not strong enough to withstand the long sea voyage—and there was no air freight then.)

## Dark Greens

The next significant mutation was the Dark Green which

The male is feeding the female. She will feed the patiently waiting baby.
HARRY LACEY

occurred in the aviaries of a famous French commercial breeder, Blanchard of Toulouse, in 1915. At the time, the possibilities of the Dark Green were not fully realized; then they were crossed with the Blues and the brilliant Cobalts (or Powder Blues, as they were first called) appeared. It seemed accidental then; today we know why. If it had not been for the original Dark Green mutation, the variety of colors would be only about a third of what it now is.

## Other Mutations

During the period from 1920 to 1939, a host of budgerigar mutations occurred: Graywings, Fallows, Grays, Slates, Opalines, Pieds. I will not go into details of their first breedings since at the present time this is of little interest, but I do discuss these varieties and how to distinguish and breed them in later chapters.

In addition to these color mutations, there are feather mutations, namely, the Crests and the Long Flights, which appeared in England in 1938. The Long Flights, although a striking mutation, are not considered worth preserving as the birds are ungainly in shape and flight. In general, they are larger, coarser versions of the slim, elegant parakeet. Nevertheless, they did at one time serve a useful purpose, and may

Birds bred for exhibition purposes, in addition to being handsome, are playful.

HORST MÜLLER

Although most pet budgerigars are kept by themselves, some people prefer pairs. While pairs often do not become attached to their owners, they do enjoy each other's company.

do so again. By judicious crossings, they were responsible for the production of certain wanted characteristics in exhibition budgerigars.

The Crested varieties now exist in three forms, namely the Full Circular, Half Circular and Tufted or Cockatiel Crest. One of the Crested mutations first appeared in North America and the second in France. Being similar, they are now interbred.

## Halfsiders (Bicolors)

Budgerigars, half one color, half another, divided right down the middle—head, breast and back—have been known since 1929 when a blue and green one was exhibited at the Crystal Palace show in London. They are not mutations since they do not breed true.

A number of eminent geneticists have studied this physical oddity. Their theories differ somewhat, and are highly complex. While other species have been known to produce half-siders, they are usually hermaphrodites, combining the two sexes; but this is not true of budgerigars.

They have been reported in white and yellow, blue and cobalt, dark green and light green, dark green and blue and light green and blue.

Tricolors also exist; these carry three distinct colors. The first one shown, in 1935, was blue, green and yellow. They are not to be confused with the Harlequins.

## Genetic Studies

No history could be considered complete without a mention of the pioneer work in the study of budgerigar genetics performed by the German scientist Dr Hans Duncker, in Bremen. Dr Duncker had the use of the large breeding aviaries of Consul-General C. H. Cremer for his experiments. Their work established the principles of color breeding on which later geneticists have been able to build. Since then, of course, a great deal of work has gone into the study of budgie inheritance. A practical summary of these discoveries is covered in Chapter XIII.

## Talking Budgies

History does not record just when or where the budgie's ability to mimic the human voice was discovered. Curiously, this amazing talent was not recognized early in their history, probably because the birds were rarely kept singly. Kept in pairs or groups, budgies seldom, if ever, repeat human speech. It was long believed they would pine away and die if not kept in pairs, and that is how the misnomer "Love Birds" came into being. We now know this to be a misunderstanding, and that lone specimens are perfectly happy—if they have human companionship. When kept alone, started young and properly trained, they are more than willing to combine their "bird language" with ours. Budgies kept in groups do not "mimic."

This baby bird will be ready for adoption in about three weeks. The permanent identification band on his leg gives the year of birth and an individual serial number.

# II Selecting a Parakeet

Choosing a parakeet is not difficult, and one should willingly invest the little time required for the selection of a healthy, active bird. The life span of a parakeet is usually six to seven years, although twelve to twenty is not uncommon, so the time spent in choosing a good parakeet is a wise initial investment that—over the years—will return a high dividend of entertainment and enjoyment.

## Color Choice

Color is the greatest single factor in the choice of a parakeet. This is true even for professional breeders. Parakeets, in fact, are classified by color, rather than by size or shape. Even feathering is a secondary factor in classification, although the feathers of a healthy bird have an observable naturally glossy sheen.

Color, however, has no influence on intelligence, hardiness or adaptability, nor does it determine a young bird's potential as a tame talking pet or a trickster, although the talents of individual birds can and do vary considerably.

Color choice is rich and varied. Most shades of normal blue, yellow, gray, green and white are available. There are "rares" and, of course, the prices for such birds are higher, but the colors available at relatively inexpensive prices are varied enough to satisfy most tastes.

In industrial towns and large cities, it might be wiser to get a bird of one of the darker shades. Although the feathers of the darker birds do, of course, become soiled, dirt does not show up as much as it does if the feathers are light.

## The Healthy Parakeet

When purchasing your parakeet, there are two initial factors that must be taken into consideration: place of purchase and cost.

One of the best ways to guarantee the purchase of a healthy, active parakeet is to approach only those sources you trust, whether it be a private breeder, a pet shop or the pet department of a variety store.

Always select a store or shop in which the animals—be they dogs, cats, birds, or anything else—are healthy and happy looking. Avoid shops or pet departments that are not kept clean and do not have a good selection of parakeets.

The black beak, the bars covering the entire head, the solid black eye and the poorly formed or unformed necklace are the markings of a baby parakeet.

Parakeets are known for their insatiable curiosity. Everything new must be investigated, and if possible played with.

One indication of general stock quality is the use of identification bands. This usually indicates that the bird was bred by a member of a budgerigar society that maintains quality standards. Once such a purchase is made, do not remove the band. It serves as a means of lasting identification and a record of the year of breeding. A note should be made of the full coding on the band, as in case the bird escapes the band will identify it.

Insofar as cost is concerned, most healthy parakeets sell for five to ten dollars, more or less; a small price to pay for years of companionship. Discount birds priced at one or two dollars are bred for quantity, not quality. Such birds are "culls"; that is, second-class specimens. Although it is true that dealers will sometimes offer quality birds at sale prices to attract new business, your chances of purchasing a healthy parakeet at such a price are minimal.

The culls from prize-winning stock are offered for sale, and they are often excellent birds; however, these culls will certainly not be sale priced. Remember, you get what you pay for, and parakeets are no exception to this rule.

Before making your purchase you must have a picture fixed in your mind, a picture of how a desirable parakeet should look. First and foremost, the youngster should be able to fly smoothly and walk rapidly without any apparent effort. A fully flighted, vigorous bird will move swiftly from place to place, but one suffering from any weakness will flutter and struggle when flying, usually while losing height. It might be thought that a young bird straight from the nest would not be able to fly well, but this is not so. I have seen birds leave the nestbox for the first time and fly twenty yards or more, straight as an arrow from a bow!

The eyes of a healthy parakeet are bright, clear and wide open. The legs are straight, with two front toes and two back toes. When balanced on a perch, a good keet sits steadily, without wobbling, and positions himself at an angle of $30°$ from the vertical. The claws grip firmly.

Generally speaking, the body and head should form a symmetrical curve, gracefully tapered from neck to tip of tail, with a straight back line. The chest is "meaty," forming a rather deep curve. The total general impression should be one of "gentle ferocity" and ease.

When selecting your parakeet there are, of course, certain factors to watch for and *avoid*. Some of the more obvious are:

**French Molt:** Some birds suffer from a feather condition known as French Molt. This is discussed in detail in Chapter XV. Although such birds may eventually grow new feathers, they should be avoided. This condition affects very young budgerigars; it can be mild or severe. In the mild cases, some or all of the long wing and tail feathers fall out; in the more severe cases, almost all of the feathers are shed. It is most unwise to keep any bird that has lost its body feathers.

Generally speaking, all the feathers should be perfect and not broken in any way. Too many broken feathers in tail or wings are a sign of weak feathering. However, broken or missing feathers will grow in again at the next molt; a tail which has been pulled out by accident will grow back within a few weeks.

**Undershot Beak:** Sometimes, because of heredity or

It's only a plastic parakeet but it does provide company. It will be snuggled up to, conversed with, kissed and nuzzled.

because of wet feeding by its parents, a young parakeet will develop an "undershot beak"; that is, the lower part of the beak protrudes out and grows up over the top part. Such a beak can, of course, be trimmed and the necessity for this operation will become even more frequent as the bird gets older. Such a bird never looks quite the same as one with a normal beak.

**Stained Vent Feathers:** Another negative sign to watch for and avoid is stained vent feathers. Such stains indicate that the bird is suffering from diarrhea. Although young birds that are handled too frequently may develop a temporary form of loose droppings, such a condition soon passes and rarely stains the vent feathers; but diarrhea is often a symptom of a more serious disease than the diarrhea itself, and the purchase of such a bird should be avoided.

## Sexing

It is difficult to determine the sex of a parakeet under three

to four months old. Even experts can make a wrong identification, but some develop a "feeling" which enables them
to make a fairly accurate guess. Generally speaking, the ceres
(the bridge of waxy flesh that surrounds the nostril at the
base of the beak) of the normal dark-eyed males are bold and
blue-tinted, whereas those of the young hens are flatter and
of a white or whitish-blue shade. When adult, the cere of
the male will be bright blue, that of the female tan, whitish
blue, buff or brown.

When it comes to sexing the red-eyed varieties and the
Recessive Pieds (Harlequins), it is much more difficult. Here
the cocks have flesh-colored ceres and many of the young hens
have ceres of a similar color. However, the ceres of the cocks
are usually much more bold and glossy.

In even more general terms, the sex of some babies is said
to be indicated by behavior. The young female is more
likely to bite than the male when first handled. Also, it is
believed that the female bites harder. Again, unlike the male,
the female baby is known to "cluck" when annoyed. Sexing
in this manner, of course, is more a matter of experience than
objective observation, and the unpracticed observer will
more than likely not find the above too helpful.

With some parakeets, however, the visual coloring is a
sure indication of the bird's sex. These are known as sex-
linked crosses. They are fully discussed in Chapter XIII. If a
baby comes from such parents, the new owner will know its
sex without doubt.

Sex, however, should not be the final determining factor
*unless* you are planning to mate your pet. The feathers of
both sexes are equally brilliant, although the male tends to
darker hues. Both male and female can be trained to talk and
do tricks, and although young females are more inquisitive
and aggressive than are the males, they are noisier and
initially shyer. It balances out. No matter which you choose,
with proper care and attention your parakeet will prove itself
a constant source of entertainment and delight.

## Age

Adult birds can be trained to talk and do tricks, but the young

HORST MÜLLER

A parakeet will amuse himself with a mirror, sometimes for hours on end. The mirror image is loved, fought, fed and sometimes caressed. A healthy parakeet will frequently regurgitate food in an attempt to feed its mirror image.

are more adaptable and are far easier to teach, because they do not, while being trained, have to "unlearn" the behavior patterns already developed in the adult. The best age for purchasing is five to six weeks, but be sure that the nestling is able to feed itself. Some learn to do so quickly, but others take well over a week after leaving the nest before they can crack the seed and fill their crops; if they are unable to, during this period the parents supplement the baby's feeding.

There are several ways to determine the age of a baby

parakeet. First, the baby's beak is black until it is five or six weeks old; it then begins to fade; at six to seven weeks the beak develops the horn color we recognize in adult parakeets. The ceres of the young are light blue and their eyes are apparently larger than those of adults because both the iris and the pupil of the young are black. At about three months the iris begins to lighten; at six months it is gray. Only the pupil remains dark for life.

The head bars, in those varieties which have them, extend from the cere all the way back into the neck. Between six and eight weeks old, as the baby goes through its first molt, these begin to disappear, starting at the front, until by three months of age the forehead and crown assume the adult coloration.

Many European cities hold open air bird markets—usually on Sundays.

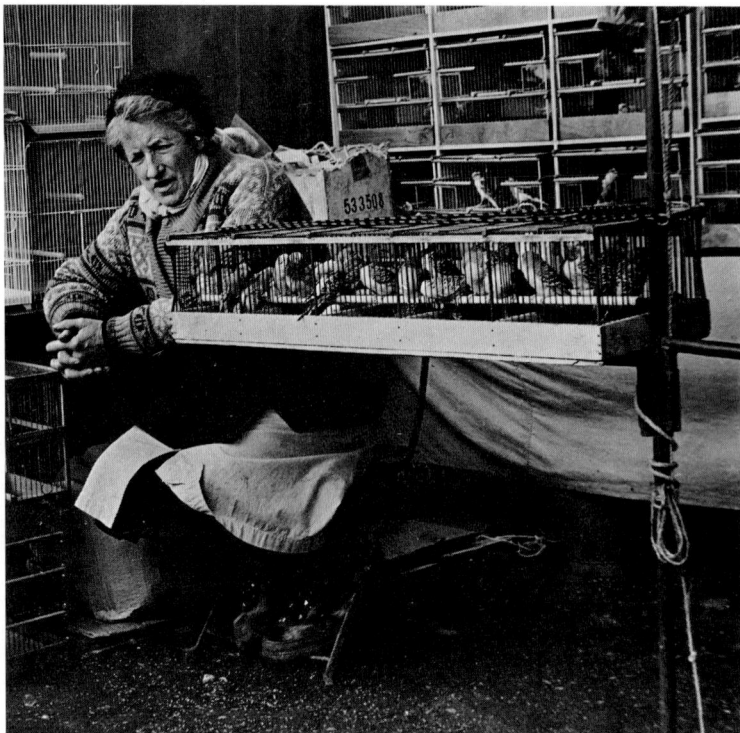

The husk or seed catcher covering the bottom of the cage can be removed for emptying. It is an aid to good housekeeping.

# III   Cages, Equipment and
# General Maintenance

It is not difficult to choose a cage for a pet parakeet. You will find all manner of styles, materials and prices at your neighborhood pet shop, in department or variety stores and, fanciest of all, at antique shops. Consider the bird first, your pocketbook second. I have known people who quibbled with a pet store owner over the price of a bird—$3.95 versus $4.95—and even settled for an older bird because it was cheaper, and then thought nothing of paying a ridiculous amount for a fancy cage.

First, invest in a good, healthy, young bird, as young as

possible if you want it to become a playful, talkative companion, and second, choose a big rectangular metal-plated cage; the bigger the better.

Consider the cage from a practical viewpoint: It should be easy to clean; the seed and water hoppers should be readily accessible to both you and the bird, and the perches should be correctly located (see page 35).

If at all possible, avoid cages that are painted or enameled. Parakeets love to nibble at the bars of their cages, and anything painted will quickly become chipped and unsightly due to rust, and the swallowed paint, even though non-toxic, is not good for the bird.

Sometimes old, discarded cages are found in attics or thrift shops. If you find one and decide to repaint it, do not use an oil or lead-based paint. Choose the type of gloss enamel sold for repainting baby cribs and children's furniture. These are not toxic. Be careful, too, that tiny globs of paint do not accumulate in corners, and that the cage is thoroughly dry before you put the bird into it.

Anything wooden can be gnawed to bits by a budgie, and curlicues and odd-shaped corners are difficult to keep clean and mite-free.

A new cage must be thoroughly washed with hot water and strong detergent. This is because metal cages are dipped in acid before they leave the factory. Be sure that the cage is completely dry before you put the bird into it.

Regardless of all else, be sure that the cage wires are set so close together that your pet cannot get his head between them. Many a budgie has escaped this way, while others, unable to complete their exit, have strangled.

## Box Cages

Some owners prefer to cage their pets in box cages; they feel that these keep the birds safe from drafts since they are closed-in on three sides, and open only in front. A cage of this type can be purchased from the pet shop, but it is not too difficult to build, if one is at all handy with tools. Cage fronts of various sizes can be purchased and fitted to these home-built boxes. Consult the advertisements in one of the cage bird

Standard dowels of various sizes, some hooks and a little ingenuity are all that are needed to make all sorts of playgrounds for your pet budgie.

magazines. Be sure that all the joints are very tight so as to avoid leaving an opening which can become a focal point for chewing; also use a hard wood for the same reason.

## Perches

The number and placement of perches in the cages is sometimes a difficult decision. I would limit them to one in front of the seed cup, one in front of the water and one near the top of the cage. This last is the one on which the bird will undoubtedly spend most of his time, since budgerigars prefer high places.

Be careful not to overcrowd the cage with perches, or to place them in such spots that the bird's droppings can foul food and water, or even in such positions that the droppings from a bird on an upper perch can foul birds on the lower perches or the perches themselves.

Nor should they all be of the same diameter; it is a good idea to vary them so that the bird can relax the tendons of his claws.

Parakeets love to bathe under running water!

A healthy parakeet's feathers are naturally oily and water resistant. As we can see, the water at first runs off in big drops. The parakeet fluffs its feathers so that the liquid can penetrate.

DONALD DAULBY

Its feathers thoroughly soaked, the bath is over and the parakeet shakes itself to remove as much water as possible.

A warm, if possible sunny, place should be provided for your pet to sit with feathers fluffed out and preen itself until dry.

DONALD DAULBY

37

Natural tree branches with the bark left on make excellent perches, if they are of willow, eucalyptus or one of the fruit-woods. Avoid any which might have been sprayed with insecticides.

## Sand Trays

The cage bottom should be fitted with a sliding metal tray which can be pulled out for easy cleaning. To protect the tray, cover it with paper cut to size and then sprinkle it with bird sand sold in pet shops; this allows the bird to pick up a certain amount of essential grit and minerals. Some people use the specially prepared sanded sheets because they ease cleaning, but I feel that the birds themselves prefer loose but clean sand. If these sheets with glued-on grit are used, extra grit should be kept in a treat cup.

To keep the bird from scattering sand and seed husks from the cage when he flutters his wings, use plastic or glass cage guards to restrain the debris, and a washable plastic seed catcher suspended around and below the cage to catch the chaff.

## Location

Considerable thought must be given to the placement of the cage, as all birds are susceptible to drafts and fumes. The bird must have ample light, but at the same time should not be placed in the full rays of the sun with no shade at all. A budgerigar enjoys sunshine, and it is beneficial to his health, but like all good things, it should not be overdone; there must always be an area of shade. As a general rule of thumb, if you would feel comfortable there, so would your parakeet.

A good location for a cage is at one side of a window where there is plenty of light, and where the bird can observe outside activity and still be out of the line of a draft. Kitchens, with their temperature variations due to the cooking activity, must be viewed with caution.

If there are no cats or dogs in the house, the cage can be set almost anywhere except in line with an outside door. If there are other pets, I feel that a special cage stand, or a hook from the ceiling or wall, is the safest way of keeping a budgie.

Ornamental wall brackets are a practical substitute for a bird stand or table top. This cage is well equipped with a landing platform, cuttle-bone, mirror and ladder. It makes a pretty picture.

These stands are made to hold variously shaped cages. They can be moved from place to place. I know many owners who continually move their pets around from room to room and outdoors in the summer, much to the bird's pleasure.

The initial cost of a cage and stand may at first seem high, but when one thinks of the years of service and pleasure they will give, the outlay is relatively small.

## Cage Covers

I am frequently asked if a budgie should be covered at night: I find that this necessity varies with the individual. Some birds like to be covered; others object to it strongly, so it is a matter for the owner and the bird to work out for themselves. After careful consideration, I think the most sensible method is to cover one side or part of the top so that no artificial light shines directly on the bird. This gives him an opportunity of

The door of this cage opens downward to form a landing platform. The grate on the bottom helps the bird keep his feet clean.

either resting under the cover or coming out to see things for himself. Some birds enjoy creeping into an open paper bag or small box laid on its side.

## Toys

A pet parakeet enjoys having a toy in his cage and there are wide selections of "keet toys" in pet shops. Too many, however, may distract the bird's attention from his owner and cause the cage to look untidy. A simple mirror, single or double sided, with a bell attached, is one of the best toys for a pet budgie. A toy ladder can also furnish amusement and exercise, but only if it does not curtail the flying space too drastically. It is a mistake to clutter up a cage with toys; it makes much more sense to establish a "playground" outside the cage where the bird can exercise daily. Beware of fine wires, strings or springs in which a budgie can entangle its neck or wings.

## Playgrounds

Playgrounds can be purchased complete with perches, ladder, swing, mirror and so on, or you can assemble your toys and build your own. A baking tin makes a good base; the equipment can be purchased in pet shops or variety stores, or made of hardwood doweling.

## Landing Platform

When the time comes for the pet to be allowed out of his cage a landing platform should be fixed at the open cage door. Such a platform makes it easy for a bird to go in and out of the cage. Many birds have difficulty trying to re-enter their cages otherwise.

## Dangers

I must stress most emphatically that *before* a bird is allowed out of its cage, all house doors and windows must be tightly closed, blinds should be drawn over windows, any open fires covered by a wire screen and all electrical appliances and stoves turned off. In hot weather, fans must be switched off or shielded in some way. If safety precautions are always observed, the bird is less likely to escape or be injured. Also, see Chapter XVI.

## Plant Hazards

Potted plants or cut flowers in the room with the free flying budgie present a danger to both bird and plant. Budgerigars are notoriously inquisitive. They invariably make a bee line for anything that is green and growing. Many species of plants and flowers are poisonous to budgerigars, and some of the spiny cacti can give nasty wounds. To rule out either of these unpleasant possibilities, never give the budgie his freedom in such a room. Remove the plants first, or cover them with plastic sheets.

Many budgies love to chew greens, and will soon shred delicate house plants.

## Cage Care

The cage and its appurtenances should be kept scrupulously clean. This includes the perches, seed, water and grit cups, the toys and the cage cover. Establish a regular cleaning routine. In the majority of cases this should happen once a week. Periodically everything should be thoroughly scoured with a strong disinfectant and hot water and then rinsed with running cold water to prevent disease.

Seed, water and grit cups, being made of glass, pottery or plastic, can become chipped or cracked. If this happens, they should be immediately replaced, since cracks or chips make ideal breeding grounds for germs. Similarly, any badly gnawed toy should be discarded.

## Baths

Wild budgerigars take baths by rolling in dew-laden grasses, but this is not always possible in captivity. Pet shops usually offer plastic or metal bird baths which can be attached to the

Do things look different from this side?

open cage door. Some birds prefer a dip in their drinking pots. Sometimes a small plug of wet growing grass or a handful of wet lettuce instead of water will be appreciated in the bath, and the owner will enjoy watching his pet's antics. A bird at liberty will often find its way into the kitchen and take a bath under the dripping faucet. When a pet has this habit, the *hot* faucet must *always* be tightly turned off. Here again, this kind of bathing will give enjoyment to the family as well as the bird!

## Keep Him Clean

While many budgies enjoy playing in water, not all like to take baths and there may come a time when you will have to give yours one; here's how. (If you are preparing him for a show, do it at least a week ahead of time.)

Bathing is done only if absolutely necessary and when it is done, great care must be exercised at every step to avoid injuring the bird.

First, make sure that you are working in a warm room, and that you have a spotlessly clean cage standing by in which to house the bird while he is drying.

Prepare two basins of warm water; dissolve a little mild dishwashing detergent in one. Take your bird gently but firmly in your hand with the thumb and forefinger pinioning his head. Dip him up and down several times in the soapy water, making sure that none gets on his head. Now take an old soft shaving brush, and brush over him, working the lather in well, stroking with the lay of the feathers—do a good job around the vent. Use an old toothbrush or a piece of soft sponge to wash the head, being extremely careful not to get water in the eyes, mouth or nostrils. Spread the wings against the side of the bowl to brush them. Use great care when cleaning the tail feathers to prevent pulling them out.

Use the second bowl for a final, thorough rinsing. Now get the bird as dry as possible by wrapping him in a warm turkish towel, and then putting him in the clean cage close by a source of heat. Keep the bird in a warm room for the rest of the day, otherwise he may take a fatal chill; but not in a spot so excessively warm that the feathers curl. A ladies'

Tail-pulling should be discouraged! It will ruin the bird's disposition.

hair dryer will hasten the drying process, but don't ever leave a budgie unattended with the heat blowing.

## Mirrors

There are arguments pro and con concerning budgerigars and mirrors. Obviously, the big mirror presents a danger to the uncaged bird who may try to fly right through. I think it is a good idea to cover all mirrors (as well as windows) the first few weeks that the budgie is allowed out.

As for small mirrors and toy mirrors, a different problem presents itself. The average budgie loves a mirror and he enjoys looking at himself in it. Many owners believe in letting their bird have a mirror when they leave him alone to keep him from loneliness.

Others believe that this encourages the bird to fall in love with his "companion" and forget his master. It is true that some budgerigars fall in love with their own image, and regurgitate food to feed it.

So, as far as I am concerned, the question remains open. I suggest that you allow a mirror until you see that it is becoming an obsession, and then remove it or cover it up with a cloth.

## Clothespins

The common spring-clamp wooden clothespin lends itself to all manner of use in the keeping of budgerigars. It can be used to hold cage doors open or shut, and to clip a number of things to cage bars: greens, carrot strips or millet sprays, for instance. Several can serve as temporary perches exactly where you want them, and to form "circular stairways" winding up from the bottom of the cage or aviary to the top, on which the budgie can play and climb. Another use is in aviaries where they can be used to fasten twiggy branches to the netting, and between nest boxes. You will undoubtedly discover still other ways of utilizing this inexpensive wooden clamp.

## Summer Care

Cleanliness, always essential, is even more important during the summer because heat can cause the rapid decay of food-stuffs, promote breeding of insects, encourage the growth of bacteria and bring on sunstroke. Consequently, all water and food vessels and the cage or aviary floor, as well as all appurtenances, must be kept hygienically clean.

If at all possible, try to give a bird who lives inside the year round some outdoor air. On pleasant days set his cage outside; not in the direct sun of course, but in a pleasant shaded area, and make sure that it is protected from meandering animals. It is not a bad idea to remove the cage-bottom, set the cage squarely on the grass and let the bird roll in it, "get his feet in the earth."

A season's breeding ready for shipment.

# IV   Aviaries and Birdrooms

The word "aviary" means, of course, any structure that can be built or converted to house birds. More often it is out-doors, but occasionally attics and cellars are converted for this purpose, and sometimes even spare bedrooms. In these cases, they're called "birdrooms." These are discussed further on.

In its simplest form, an aviary consists of a building in which the birds find shelter from the elements, and a screened-in outdoor area in which they can fly to their heart's content. From here on when I refer to the "shelter," I speak of this weatherproofed outbuilding, and when I use the word "flight," I mean the open outdoor area. Together, they form the aviary.

If you can afford it, the shelter itself can become a pleasant birdroom, spacious enough for you to enter and work in, to move around and even sit down. In this case, there will be inside flights, as well as the outside one that I am about to describe.

Usually, the flight will occupy more space than the shelter, although there are no hard and fast rules about this. The consensus is that approximately 80% of the available site should be assigned to the flight, 20% to the shelter.

While the shelter can be comparatively small (depending on the number of birds) the flight should be as large as you can build it. If possible, it should measure no less than eight feet long, four feet wide and six feet high. The important dimension is length. The birds need it to fly—and fly they must if they are to get their needed exercise and be in condition to breed. The entire aviary should be divided right down the middle—shelter and flight—so that the cocks and hens can be separated until you are ready to breed them. At least, they should be, if you intend to control their breeding. If you just want an aviary filled with pretty birds, no separation is necessary and the birds can breed "at will." This latter method is known as Colony breeding, as compared to the former, Controlled breeding.

I would suggest that the novice who is planning to engage in serious breeding start with no more than six pairs. It does not follow, however, that the aviary or birdroom should be planned to accommodate no more than this, since your budgerigar populace will start to "explode" almost immediately.

## Planning the Aviary

More likely than not, if it is home-built, the aviary will be constructed of wood. There is nothing wrong with wood, except that parakeets are great nibblers and chewers, and anything less than an oak beam can ultimately be reduced to shreds. So, in planning a flight, which is usually built on

An excellent birdroom and aviary constructed by an amateur but competent handyman. The building is of cinder block, faced with stucco, 16 feet by 9 feet. The flight is 9 feet by 4 feet by 6 feet high.

wood frames, staple your wire netting to the inside of the wood.

Although outdoor aviaries are usually designed for large-scale breeding, they can, with little planning, be made quite attractive, as several of the pictures on these pages illustrate. They can be designed and painted to match the owner's house or the surrounding outbuildings. The perches, inside and out, can be of natural wood with the bark left on, as indicated in Chapter III, or dead trees can be installed. The whole thing can be landscaped to your own taste. I would like to point out, however, that because of the budgerigar's gnawing habit, it is difficult to get trees, bushes or shrubs to grow in a flight. When any buds appear, the birds quickly nibble them off. However, grass, short or tall, can be grown and made to look attractive and, when wet, will provide the birds with a natural bath.

Their nibbling habit also makes it almost impossible to grow vines up the sides of the flight netting, although they can be grown on windbreaks a few inches from the mesh.

Some very attractive and convenient outdoor aviaries

have been built in the corners formed by ells and angles of
the owner's house. This saves constructing two walls—these
two walls will always be warm in winter—and if a house
window opens onto the area, it permits using the window sill
for a feeding shelf without going outside in bad weather.
The house windows, too, will give a picturesque view of the
birds.

## Locating the Aviary

First of all, consider access for yourself, remembering that
the birds will have to be cared for summer and winter.
Remember too that you will want to enjoy watching the
birds in the flight, so there should be a comfortable sitting
area, and it should be a pleasant spot, not an eye-sore. You
will want a site that is protected from the worst aspects of
weather—cold winds, hot sun and rain dripping from trees.
In winter you will want sunshine; in summer you will be

Given an adequate supply of the essentials such as food, grit and water,
budgerigars will do quite well even in less than professional looking
aviaries.

HARRY LACEY

needing shade. Budgies like a little of both, so locate your aviary in such a spot that part of the flight is in the sun and part of it shaded.

Generally speaking, the aviary should face the south-west, but with a flight open on three sides this is not too easy; I would suggest having the shelter's windowless side facing the prevailing wind. If your flight is to be in an exposed area, it might be wise to board up one of the sides, if not two. If there are strong winds, windbreaks should either be built or planted, but, in the case of planting, do not have any trees so close to the aviary that water can drip off their leaves.

Easy access to a water connection will make things easier and you will also have to anticipate drainage.

**Shelter Construction**

The shelter should be raised off the ground if at all possible, to discourage rats, mice and other animals from taking up their abode beneath it. It is a good idea to prefabricate the

HARRY LACEY

Inexpensive plastic bins will keep your seeds and other foods clean, dry and safe from vermin.

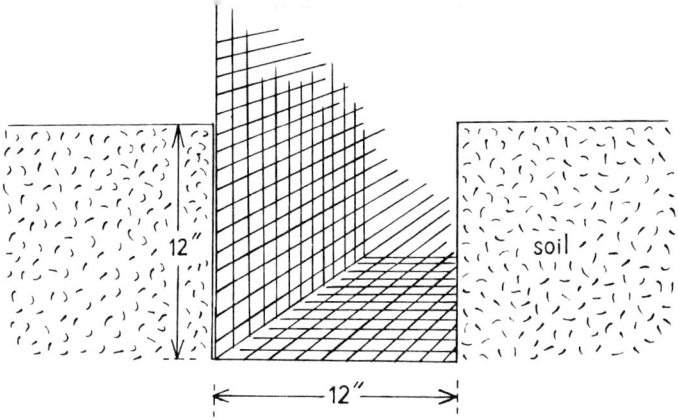

Vermin-proofing an aviary.

MICHAEL YOUENS

floor of the shelter, as well as the walls and roof, at a convenient working spot like the floor of a barn or garage, and then assemble them at the site.

The floor should be constructed of one-inch thick tongue and groove planks, abutted closely. They should then be swabbed with a good wood preservative such as creosote, and covered with half-inch wire netting. This netting, which should be stapled to the *underside* of the floor, should be wide enough to extend beyond the four sides for six or eight inches. After the floor is laid on its supporting piles (and the walls assembled), this mesh should be turned up at right angles and stapled to the outside of the building. (Plaster lath nailed along the edges of the wire net is usually more satisfactory than stapling.)

The walls can be built of 2 × 4 framing, reinforced with horizontal crosspieces, and should be as high as possible, since parakeets like to roost high when they sleep. The framing can be covered with plywood, sealed and protected against bad weather. It is a good idea to keep in mind the standard plywood panel, 4 × 8, as a basic module when "blueprinting" your shelter. In some climates, heating will have to be supplied, although if the aviary is draft-free budgerigars can be acclimated to very cold weather.

## Shelter Roof

The roof should slant, with the lower, water-dripping end away from the flight, and it should be carefully weather-

The interior of a breeding room. The screened flight at the left is used for youngsters or cocks during the off-season. The nest boxes are on the outside, and hinged for easy access. The cards are for noting the identification numbers of the cock and hen, as well as important dates and records. While this breeder does not clean out the cages during the breeding season, a handful of new sawdust is added weekly. The water tubes are on the outside so that they can be easily refilled, with drinking spouts projecting into the cage.

proofed with standard roofing materials to keep out rain and snow. A roof that extends a foot or so beyond the sides will be more protective, and if it is more than a tiny shelter, rain gutters and spout should be provided.

## Doors

You will need a door into the shelter and one leading from the shelter into the flight. You will not need a door opening directly into the flight; in fact, such a door, unless it is carefully planned, can be hazardous because it will enable the birds to fly out as you go in. This is also an ever-present danger in the door you will use to enter the shelter; the best safety device is a vestibule and double doors: open and close the first door before opening and closing the second. Lacking space for a vestibule, hang a screen door *inside* the door frame, opening in, while the wooden door opens out. All doors should be low—about four feet—since disturbed birds (and they panic when you enter) tend to fly upward.

## Windows

Even though there is an open flight, there should be as much light inside the shelter as possible. Use two walls for windows (but not opposite walls), the other two for roosts, feeders, drinkers and nest boxes. One window should face the pop-holes, so that its light will help to attract reluctant budgies back inside at dusk. Netting should, of course, guard the windows, but they should be glass and capable of being opened in pleasant weather. Remember too to provide ventilation for those times when the windows must be kept closed, and in planning vents and windows, keep in mind the fact that there should be no drafts. Be careful about using plastic windows. A new ultraviolet-retarding ingredient being put into plastic and fiberglass to stop sun rot may be the cause of clear eggs. Ultraviolet light activates the glands responsible for reproduction.

## Popholes

You may well ask how the birds get from the shelter into the flight. One often hears about bobholes or popholes opening from one to the other, but in my opinion these openings are usually too small. They can cause the birds, particularly the young ones, to damage their wings when going through,

Details of the nesting box. This breeder uses sawdust, rather than the usual concave block. The 2-inch by 3-inch block on the right is just under the entry hole and serves as a landing platform.

Top: An ornamental aviary with an outside flight. Center: The inside of an aviary without outside flights. Below: Floor plan of indoor aviary.

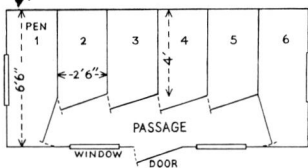

MICHAEL YOUENS

or prevent them from finding their way back into the shelter. In my experience the popholes should be no less than 12 inches square. With these, the birds can fly, not hop, through. For a six-foot aviary, I usually cut three of these holes, as high as possible, each with its own platform and a sliding door, so that the birds can all be shut inside when necessary.

If glass is used for these doors, it should be covered with wire mesh to prevent the birds from trying to fly through it. Any exposed wire edges should be covered with strips of wood to keep the birds from being scratched.

## The Flight

The flight should be open to the sky except where it joins the shelter; here two or three feet of the flight should be roofed over to protect the popholes and landing deck. As I have already stated, the flight should be as long as possible, length being even more important than height.

## Flight Floor

I prefer concrete for the floor of the flight; it is the most practical, easiest to keep clean, and therefore, hygienic; but I am willing to admit that an earthen floor is more natural, and conducive to decorative planting. The disadvantage of a dirt floor is obvious—the accumulation of droppings and filth which can breed disease. It is for this reason that some aviculturists build portable flights (and shelters) that can be moved once a year.

The concrete floor is standard, and you will find directions for laying one in almost any home construction manual. Remember to embed bolts into the still-soft concrete to which the sidewall uprights can be attached, and to provide for drainage. If you are going to use concrete, the floor of the shelter can be laid at the same time, obviating the wood flooring already described.

A baby Yellow-face Cinnamon Sky Blue and a Yellow-face Cinnamon Cobalt. Both are Opalines. Blue-series birds with yellow faces have surpassed the Blues with white faces in popularity.

HARRY LACEY

Kept in an outdoor aviary of soft-billed birds, this Lutino cock and Opaline Sky Blue hen raised two nests of youngsters.

Use a good concrete sealer before allowing the birds in.

In case you decide on the earthen floor, here is a way to handle it which many breeders recommend. Measure the flight area and dig an excavation to a depth of about eight inches, saving the soil. Now cover the excavation with a layer of broken glass, and over the layer of glass, spread the finest mesh size of wire netting, again using enough wire (as in the shelter) to turn it up at right angles to join the netting that forms the three sides (the shelter will form the fourth wall). Now refill the excavation with the removed dirt and roll it down hard. Around the edges erect your flight walls, turning up the floor mesh to join them on the inside. About once a year (or sooner if there is any kind of contagious disease) the dirt of this floor can be dug up, disposed of and replaced.

## Floor Covering

Both concrete and wooden floors need some sort of covering and for this purpose fine gravel, clean coarse sand, coarse pine sawdust or a mixture of all these can be used. The sand used for cat boxes is a good absorbent material. These should be raked over periodically and all unsanitary debris removed.

Some breeders treat the bare ground with unslaked lime, raking it in and watering it immediately. The birds, of course, should be kept in the shelter while this is being done, and not allowed out until the next morning.

In the outdoor flight, sand or gravel can be put into trenches directly beneath the perches to catch the droppings; this makes cleaning up that much easier.

## Sides

In building the framework of your flight, use 2 × 4s and horizontal crosspieces (using as few horizontal bars as possible, so as not to obstruct your vision of the birds); cover these with wire netting either stapled firmly or held down by plaster lath. Stretch the net on the *inside* of the uprights to protect the wood from being gnawed. If the netting is painted with a black non-toxic outside paint it will become virtually invisible.

## Flight Roof and Cat Guards

The wire mesh, of course, will be spread across the top, and it is a good idea to use the finest mesh netting available. It will help to keep out leaves and other wind-blown debris, as well as cats' paws. If the flight is built long and narrow, it will facilitate stretching the net and keep it from sagging; otherwise, the roof will have to be built in paneled sections like window screens, laid across and bolted or hinged together.

To keep cats and other preying animals off the roof of the flight, cat guards—about a foot of netting sticking out from the four sides like the brim of a hat—should line the edges. In situating the aviary, avoid any tree limbs which would enable animals to jump down on the flight.

## Rats and Mice

Mice, since they can crawl through very fine mesh, are always a problem in the outdoor aviary. Rats are too in some areas, but they are usually easier to keep out. Rats will kill birds; mice are attracted by the seeds, and have been known to attack baby birds. The best way to keep mice out—rats can even gnaw through concrete—is to sink sheets of corrugated metal into the ground to a depth of 12 inches and up the sides of the flight and shelter for 18 inches, including any doors. Rat guards should be affixed at all corners. Perhaps a dog and cat roaming the premises is the best answer. Dishes containing a rodenticide may be kept under the raised portion of the aviary where the birds can't reach it, but be sure it is also out of the reach of dogs and cats.

## Water

The best watering system for an outdoor aviary is a water faucet or a garden hose from which water is allowed to drip, drop by drop, into a clay saucer protected from droppings.

## Birdrooms

Almost any spare room, attic, dry basement, sun porch or barnloft can be turned into a birdroom simply by putting wire netting across the windows, and sand and grit on a tarpaulin spread over the floor, with double screen doors for access. Install a small dead tree (not an evergreen) for perches, place food hoppers and drinkers in such a way that they cannot be fouled by droppings—and you're in business. Allow about seven square feet for each pair of budgies. This setup will, of course, lead to colony breeding when, at stated seasons of the year, you hang high the nest boxes; be sure, however, to install more nest boxes than you have pairs since often two females—like women the world over—are bound to want the same nest.

Of course, in the more carefully planned birdroom,

especially the one intended for controlled breeding, the whole room will not be an open flight. There will be shelves for breeding cages with a clearance of about 18 inches. Start with the bottom shelf, which should be a convenient working height from the floor, and do not go so high that you cannot see into the cages on the top "floor."

One end of the room, preferably the end with windows protected by netting, should be fenced off into a flight area, divided into male and female sections. Here the young parakeets can be loosed and here the breeders can be kept when they are not nesting. It goes without saying that natural wood perches will be included, as well as appropriate seed hoppers, drinkers, grit and so on, not only in the flights, but in the breeding cages as well.

The other end of the room should contain a work table, cabinets and drawers for storage and records. If at all possible, running water should be introduced. Draft-free ventilation and heat must also be provided; 70°F is a good average heat, although it can drop to 50° or go up to 90° for short periods without causing any harm.

If artificial light is to be provided use fluorescent lighting with an automatic timer.

A very well-bred Gray Green cock. An excellent father, five of his offspring have won show awards.

When two keets bill and coo like this—

# V Feeding and Nutrition

In the wild state, budgerigars feed on a wide variety of grass seeds, ripe and unripe. In fact, they are called Grass Parakeets because of this. It should, however, be constantly borne in mind that what is appropriate for the bird in its free state is not necessarily suitable (or always available) under captive conditions. In the wild, birds can vary their food at will and, of course, do burn up calories at a tremendous rate with the amount of energy they expend foraging and escaping predators. Captive birds are housed in restricted quarters, protected

—it soon means two fine babies like these.

from the elements and danger and seldom have the opportunity to get nearly enough natural exercise.

This being so, their food should be so controlled that they cannot eat highly fattening foods, which also causes problems other than overweight. I believe that over-rich feeding does contribute in many cases to feather problems. Birds kept in large outdoor aviaries with plenty of flying space will, of course, need more of the energy producing foods than their caged brothers. It follows then that the purpose for which a parakeet is kept—exhibition, pet, liberty or breeding—will govern its diet. Age, too, enters into it. A nestling or growing bird requires a different diet than the adult.

## Basic Diet

White canary seed *(Phalaris canariensis)* and millet *(Panicum miliaceum)* form the basis for all budgerigar diets. The birds de-husk these seeds and swallow the kernels whole. In tests made with seeds already husked, the budgies preferred the unhusked seed. While these two seeds are most preferred, the birds will enjoy, in more limited quantities: wheat, oats, rice, milo, corn (maize), buckwheat, rape, flax, hemp and sesame, among others.

Aside from these seeds, the budgie should also have small amounts of leaf greens, vegetables and one or more supplements—these last are commercially prepared concentrates of many foods, with the emphasis on their vitamin and mineral content.

## Packaged Mixtures

For those who maintain only a few birds, it makes sense to purchase the prepared parakeet (not canary) seed mixtures put out by reputable birdseed packagers. It is pointless to buy in quantity, or mix your own formulas, because by the time the seed is used up, it will be stale.

Most seed mixes consist of a blend of equal amounts of canary seed and millet. For young birds, a higher percentage of canary seed is indicated because it is easier to crack. Buy a half pound or a pound of plain canary seed (not mixed Canary Food) and increase the proportion of this seed in your pre-packaged mixture by 10 or 15%. If your young budgie does have difficulty cracking seeds, it is a good idea to go over them first with a rolling pin (cracking, not crushing them).

## Quantity Mixtures

Obviously, if a great many birds are to be fed, seed should be purchased in quantity and mixed to your own requirements since it cuts down on waste, as well as expense. The 50%-50% formula given for the packaged mixtures is recommended.

The kind of millet usually used is white or proso, sometimes called broomcorn or hog millet. This is more nutritious than the yellow. Red millet is not included since some people believe that budgies have trouble digesting it. (This belief has been questioned in recent years and today many of the large commercial firms include some red millet in their mix since the birds seem to enjoy it.) Millet seeds should be large, smooth and creamy white or very light yellow. Canary seeds should be plump, shiny and smooth.

If you mix your own seed, you should still buy in fairly small quantities in order to make sure that the seed remains fresh. Sift through it to be certain it is free of foreign matter, chaff, dust and, particularly, vermin droppings. The husks should shine; the seed should be plump. The mixture should be kept in porous cloth bags or open containers in a dry place. Seeds must never be deprived of air.

There is no point in buying cheap seed. It is cheap, more often than not, because it has never been cleaned or because it is stale. Stale seed has no nutritional value; the embryo must be "alive." Seed can, of course, be tested by planting it in a flower pot to see what percentage germinates. If it is low, discard the seed and buy fresh.

Two sprays of millet, a food which is enjoyed as a treat by budgies. Cuttlebone not only supplies needed calcium, but it also helps keep a budgie's beak worn down.

## Spray Millet

Millet seed grows in sprays; normally it is threshed for the package mixtures, but parakeets enjoy eating millet still on the stalk. These stalks are obtainable from pet shops, usually packaged in plastic to keep them clean and fresh. Hang a spray in your pet's cage, or hang several in the aviary, but do not consider it as part of the bird's basic diet; it is more of a treat and should be offered two or three times a week. It can also be used as a reward when training the bird.

Millet spray is sometimes soaked in water until it starts to germinate, but I prefer to feed mine in the natural dry form.

## Oats and Groats

Most budgies like groats, rolled oats or clipped whole oats, but these should not be given too often. Because they are fattening, they are not always included in a basic seed mixture; they should be offered in a treat cup. Groats are oats from which the husks have been removed. They are also known as hulled oats. Whether to feed groats instead of oats is debatable. Adult budgies can crack the husk of the oat just as easily as they crack their other seed. Newly harvested oats obviously contain more moisture; groats, on the other hand, are almost always prepared from top quality oats. They are especially good for parent birds while feeding their young, so they should be added to the diet during the breeding season.

## Hemp Seed

It may come as news to some of my readers that hemp seed *(Cannabis sativa)* and marijuana seed are one and the same. In the USA, Federal law prohibits its sale unless it has been devitalized (made infertile), and in some of the states even devitalized seed cannot be sold. I mention this only because some books on bird-cage maintenance suggest that hemp seed is a highly desirable food for budgerigars, and so it is, but less so when it has been devitalized. It is high in fat and protein, so it must be given in small quantities only.

## Daily Food Consumption

The bird's digestive system is designed to supply it with enough energy to fly. To maintain this high energy expenditure, birds need a constant supply of nourishment. They assimilate their food rapidly; their digestive tract is short and food passes through it in a few hours. Some 90% of the food intake is digested and absorbed. It is truly said: a bird never stops eating. Some people's low consumption of food has prompted the saying, "He eats like a bird." If a man were to eat like a bird, he would consume 45 pounds of food in a day. A budgerigar consumes nearly 100 times its own weight in a year.

Parakeets will starve to death if they are deprived of food for 48 hours. This is why it is so important to feed them every day, and why it is so particularly important to be sure that what appears to be seed in the cup is not merely a pile of empty husks, and that if a new mixture is introduced, the bird is eating it.

The amount the budgie eats varies; the individual age, size, season of the year are among the factors that influence it. Some eat as little as a teaspoonful of seed a day; others eat four. It usually ranges from one to two teaspoonsful a day.

It is virtually impossible to estimate the amount of seed a pet bird eats because there is so much waste. A better way to measure food consumption is to count the bird's droppings. A healthy bird passes from 40 to 60 droppings every 24 hours. If fewer than 40 are passed, he is probably not eating as much as he should. Less than 30 droppings is a bad sign. See my discussion of droppings in Chapter XV.

Contrary to some so-called expert opinion, a sick bird should never be fasted. Quite the contrary—it should be tempted to eat as much as it will. This, too, is discussed more fully in Chapter XV.

## Cleaning Seed Cups

A careful watch must be kept on the bird's seed cup. It

The Green is so much smaller that it might almost be an import of a wild bird from Australia. The size difference could be due either to heredity or nutrition.

is far safer to empty it completely each day than to dump fresh seed in on top of the old. There have been many instances of budgies starving to death because their owners didn't realize that there was no seed in the cup. Budgies crack the seed, extract the kernel and let the husk drop. More often than not, it drops back into the cup, and since husked seeds look much like fresh ones, the novice thinks the cup is still full.

Even some owners who realize this fact neglect to empty the cup completely. They blow the layer of chaff off the top and add more seed. This, obviously, allows the seed at the bottom to get stale, because the bird is always eating off the top.

The best method is to empty the seed cup onto a sheet of newspaper. Blow all the chaff away. Make sure the remaining seed is clean. Clean the cup, making sure that it is thoroughly dry. Refill with fresh seed, and then, on top, place the seed salvaged from the day before. In this way, yesterday's seed will be eaten first. Budgies should have seed in front of them at all times, since they eat little and often.

**Green Leaf Foods**

A diet of seeds is not enough. The budgerigar also needs fresh green food and fruit to supply plant protein, essential vitamins and minerals, as well as cellulose for roughage. There are any number of green foods that are suitable. You will quickly discover that your bird has likes and dislikes, so at first you will have to offer various greens to find the ones he prefers.

**Wild Plants**

If you live in the country or suburbs you will undoubtedly have access to most of the following herbs, all of which parakeets will eat. You will make sure, of course, that all greens are thoroughly washed.

| | |
|---|---|
| Dandelion greens | Alfalfa |
| Chickweed | Lawn grass |
| Plantain | Teazle |
| Shepherd's purse | Clover |
| Sowthistle | Rye grass |

As for other wild plants, seeds and berries, my advice is to go easy on them unless you know what you are feeding. Too many are poisonous; just to name a few: locust, corn cockle, vetch, cottonseed, crotalaria, daubentonia, death-camus, milkweed, nightshade, lily of the valley, oleander. Among houseplants, any of the philodendrons and geraniums.

Among the edible greens, spinach stands first. Nutritional experts say the bright green leaf—when freshly cut—tops nearly all vegetables in all-around nutritive values. It contains the most iron and Vitamin A of all the common vegetables, plus above-average amounts of Vitamin C and calcium. Other leaf greens that most parakeets enjoy include:

| | |
|---|---|
| Carrot tops | Broccoli |
| Beet tops | Romaine lettuce |
| Chicory | Celery leaves |
| Watercress | Escarole |
| Cabbage leaves | Kale |
| Endive | Savoy cabbage |
| Brussels sprouts | |

Of the root vegetables, I have found that budgies like carrots best; only a few will eat turnips, beets or parsnips. Some birds like their carrots grated; others prefer to nibble at a chunk stuck through the bars of their cage.

Pots of growing greens that can be clipped to cages are available in pet shops.

## Feeding Greens

Greens should be fed once a day, but they should not be left in the cage for more than an hour or so. Be careful when first feeding them. If your budgie is not accustomed to them, he may get diarrhea, so offer small quantities every other day at first.

All greens must be fresh and clean. It is better to feed none at all than to feed crushed or wilted ones.

Always feed fresh young leaves, making sure that they are carefully washed. Any trace of possible pesticide must be removed. I cannot emphasize this too strongly. It applies equally to purchased greens and to those picked "wild."

## Home Grown Greens

If you really want to economize, you can grow your own greens. You can plant the "sweepings" from the bottom of your cages; these almost invariably contain uneaten canary and millet seeds and "fertilizer." Simply rake open a bare patch of garden, sprinkle the seeds, the chaff and the droppings over the ground and press them down with your foot. You will have a crop of "greens" in no time, guaranteed fresh. Or put a handful in a clay saucer, with a layer of damp burlap over them. The greens will grow right through the loose weave. A small and inexpensive kit to grow your own greens is available in bird stores.

One budgie lover I know grows his own carrot tops. He slices about a quarter of an inch off the tops of fresh carrots and floats these chunks in water. In a few days fresh new tops begin to sprout, and these fresh succulent greens are his birds' delight.

## Reluctant Eaters

Some birds, when first offered greens, do not want them. If your budgie is one of these, soak the greens in water first a few minutes before offering them. A few hours earlier, remove the water cup. If he is especially stubborn, remove the water cup two hours before offering them and allow the moist greens to hang. Do this as often as necessary. Once a keet has tasted greens, he will grow to like them.

## Fruit

Along with seeds and greens, you can offer fruit occasionally. Apple seems to be the most popular, although individual birds have been known to enjoy grapefruit, orange, banana, grape, pineapple, fig or pear. The fruit, especially in winter when it is expensive, may be dried. A bit of millet from a spray is always a welcomed tidbit; this can be used as a reward when training. Never let uneaten fruit remain in the cage or aviary overnight; it can rot too quickly. Too much fruit can cause diarrhea.

## Vitamin Supplements

Budgerigars need vitamin and mineral supplements to their

routine diet. This is particularly true if they are not getting strictly fresh greens, and when they are breeding. Seeds are deficient in certain vitamins; greens contribute limited amounts, but the growing bird and the breeding bird need more. Store-bought supplements are wholesome mixtures, containing all or some of the following: dried egg yolk, dried bakery products, alfalfa leaf meal, milk protein, iodized salt, parsley flakes, wheat germ, yeast, vitamins A, D and B-complex, soy grits, teazle, anise, vegetable oil, oyster shell, dried whey and, in some brands, seed to make the mixture more appetizing.

It is much easier and safer to feed the commercial "treat" foods and conditioners than to try to concoct your own, unless, of course, you have a great many birds. Do not be misled by the name "treat." These mixtures are not to be served as treats, but as a regular supplement to the diet.

The budgie's reaction to these foods sometimes borders on the miraculous. Too many people acquire budgerigars as gifts or prizes, and know nothing about their care except to give them seed and water. Soon their new pets start to waste away, grow thin and listless, and appear to lose all interest in life. But within a few days after the right minerals and vitamins have been added to their diet, they perk up, their eyes clear, the feathers take on a shine and they start "living up a storm." Liquid multivitamins are available. As budgies drink little water, these may be added to the seed. How much the bird will actually ingest that way is questionable, but it may do some good; better to mix a drop or two with soft foods.

### Codliver and Wheat Germ Oil

If you do not use one of the commercial supplements, you will have to give your growing budgies codliver oil, fortified with a few drops of wheat germ oil. This is good for the older birds too, especially in the winter and when they are raising their young. The fish oils are rich sources of vitamins A and D, the latter necessary to ensure proper utilization of calcium. Wheat germ oil contains vitamin E.

The oil can be administered in two ways: if you have

Lunchtime in a commercial aviary, where food must be prepared in bulk.

a great many birds, a teaspoonful can be added to a pound of seed. The oil should be put in a glass jar, the seed added and the jar shaken vigorously to coat the seed. The jar should then be covered and kept refrigerated; otherwise the oil may go rancid. This method is the one commonly followed, but it has its weakness in that budgies, while they take the seed into their beaks and get traces of oil, discard the coated husk and so waste most of it. The owner, not realizing this, thinks the bird is getting its full oil ration, when in reality it is not. A better method is to put drops of oil on bits of bread in a treat cup and let the bird get its quota from that.

Take warning, though, that too much fish oil is potentially dangerous. Some breeders believe that it is one of the causes of sterility, while current veterinary research seems to indicate that high levels of vitamin A predispose budgerigars to French Molt. See page 217.

**Added Protein**

Many aviculturists believe that ailments such as French Molt or tumors (discussed in Chapter XV) are caused by a lack of animal protein, and that parrots and parakeets should be given a limited amount of this in their diet regularly. Ground or chopped meat, either fresh or from a can of all-meat dog food, can be offered as a supplement every other day. If the bird will not eat meat voluntarily, try offering it in tiny bits by hand.

If you maintain flights of budgerigars, use chick starter ration for this purpose. This is a high protein food designed for poultry raisers and is obtained at feed stores. Not all birds will eat it at first, but they can be tempted to do so by mixing it with sieved hard-boiled egg and grated carrot.

Egg yolk is also rich in animal protein. Boil an egg for 15 minutes, then sieve the yolk and add to it grated carrot and two tablespoons of one of the store-bought strained baby meats.

Budgies are usually quite conservative when it comes to trying new things, including new foods. Try mixing a little of the mash with his regular seeds. Over a period of days, decrease the seeds and increase the soft food, and soon you will find him taking the mash willingly.

## Salt

A few grains of iodized salt should be added to the drinking water each day, to supply the tiny amount of iodine necessary to any active budgie.

## Bark and Sod

Budgies love to peel and eat tree bark, especially that from fruitwood trees—apple, cherry, peach, pear—as well as willow, eucalyptus and maple. Give them the branch and let them strip the rich, nutritious bark themselves. They'll enjoy it, and it is good for them—it gives them vitamins, minerals and the organic compounds essential for nutrition.

A plug of lawn sod is good, too. It should be from one to two inches thick, and placed in the cage or aviary upside down so that the birds can get to the roots and the dirt itself. Clean earth has medicinal value.

## Gravel and Grit

Since the chief part of a budgie's diet is hard seed, it is essential to supply the bird with an ample quantity of mixed grit or gravel to help digest it. Budgerigars, like all birds, lack teeth, and "mastication" is performed internally in an organ known as the gizzard. The gizzard retains a quantity of these sharp-edged grits. The swallowed seeds go first into the crop, and then by degrees into the gizzard. There it is ground so that it can be assimilated. By constant grinding, these bits of gravel lose their sharp edges, wear down and are passed along and out of the body. Naturally, they must be replaced if the bird is to be kept in first rate condition, so it is necessary to always have a cup of mixed grit in the cage.

Grit and gravel can, of course, be purchased already packed in pet shops. Be sure you buy the type intended for parakeets; canary grit is too fine. Mixing your own, if you have only one or two birds, is not worth the trouble. Never even think of gathering it from the driveway or roadside; it will be impregnated with oil, pesticide and all manner of foul matter. A good home formula consists of:

> 1 part crushed oyster shell
> 1 part clean ocean sand or river sand
> Boiled eggshell pulverized in a mixer
> or food grinder.

If a bird is to digest its food properly and stay in good health,

Budgies drink very little water, but that should be fresh and clean.

it should always have grit available. This can be sprinkled on the floor of the cage, or kept in a treat cup. Do not depend entirely on the kind of cage bottom paper that is impregnated with gravel.

## Cuttlefish Bone

This supplies the calcium the body needs and helps to keep the bird's beak worn down. It does *not* take the place of grit. Cuttlebone is the dried skeleton of the cuttlefish, and it is almost pure calcium carbonate. The bones come with holders so that they can be attached to the cage bars with the soft side of the bone toward the bird. Since some birds don't go for cuttlebone, mineral blocks are available. It was once thought that minerals were needed only when the bird was molting, but this is not so; they are needed throughout the bird's life. If you have reason to believe that the bird is not nibbling at the bone or mineral block, try scraping particles of it onto the bottom of the cage. The whole pieces are better, however, since the birds' beaks are kept in better condition by the exercise.

## Table Scraps

Throughout this chapter I have tried to emphasize the importance of correct feeding, and I want to end by stressing that most household scraps should be avoided. Starchy, spicy or greasy fried foods are strictly not for the birds. Cake, biscuits, sugar and potatoes should also be kept out of their diet. I am well aware that many budgies enjoy eating at the table with their owners, and drinking too—alcoholic beverages, no less! My advice is to not feed them the dinner menu, but offer them bits of wholewheat bread or millet spray.

## Water

Nature, in her evolutionary process, apparently decided that the budgerigar could get along on very little water—which was helpful since it is native to the semi-arid regions of

Australia. Budgies normally drink far less water than canaries —about 20% as much.★ In hot weather, however, they may drink quite freely. A lack of water will suppress appetite, egg production and activity.

Be sure the cup is placed in such a way that it cannot be fouled by droppings. The vessel should be kept scrupulously clean. Give fresh water at least once a day. Never add fresh water to the old; clean the cup every time before refilling it. Cage-bird drinkers are available in pet shops. They are a wise investment because they guard against water pollution. Suspect a bird which suddenly starts drinking a lot of water for no obvious reason of having a health problem.

**Sea Water**

Those who live close to the ocean are especially fortunate. Sea water contains just about every mineral your budgie needs; only calcium is lacking. It must be genuine sea water, however, not just a saline solution, and it must be fresh. A supply will keep about a week. However, sea water is too salty to feed undiluted, so dilute it with tap water—a tablespoon of sea water to an 8-ounce cup of tap water.

Soak a day's ration of seeds in this solution overnight, drain it in a sieve the next morning, and allow it to dry in the sun. Another method is to add the same proportion of sea water to the drinking water; the drawback to this, however, is that budgies drink so little water.

**Coprophagy**

When the parakeet's diet is deficient in calcium, it is quite likely to eat its own droppings. This unattractive habit is known as coprophagy. Calcium, of course, is present in seeds, but its chief supplemental source is the cuttlebone and the mineral block. If your bird does develop this habit, try a different seed mixture and check to see that he is nibbling cuttlebone.

★ Two budgies in a laboratory experiment were reported in good health after going 130 days without water.

All it takes to teach a bird to "kiss" is a hungry subject and a few seeds on your lips.

# VI   Taming and Training

Let me begin by stating that plumage color has no influence whatsoever on a bird's potential as a tame talking pet. There is no such thing as a "strain of talkers" as determined by color. All colors are the same in this respect. It is true that some individuals will perform better than others, but there is no way of distinguishing the exceptionally talented bird from the merely acceptable one.

Nor is it true that only male parakeets can be taught to speak. Females can be taught to talk, and some of them develop extensive vocabularies. However, many fanciers are of the opinion that males are preferable as potential talkers, although there is no scientific basis for this prejudice.

As I have already said, it is best to choose a very young parakeet if you want to train a bird to talk. A young bird is more open to suggestion and imitation than is an old one. A young bird is like a clean recording tape: it will play back what you repeat into it. For this reason, it is best to isolate the parakeet from his fellows, even canaries, for if you fail to do so, the bird will imitate the sounds of the other birds, rather than your voice. In short, control as well as you are able the "input of information" that your bird is exposed to. Almost any parakeet will learn to talk if properly trained, but your chances of success are greatly improved if you start when the bird is very young.

## First Night Home

Two questions I am frequently asked are: (1) How to transport a young parakeet to its new home, and (2) How to help the bird adapt to its new environment.

The safest means of transporting a bird is to make use of a small cardboard box, not the bird's wire cage. If a bird is put into a cage and covered up, it will inevitably flutter about wildly and hurt itself. However, when using a small box, make sure the air holes are not covered over by labels, and put plenty of seed inside. A parakeet will eat even in the dark. Because of this, it can travel long distances by auto, air or rail in boxes or show cages without coming to any harm—if it has plenty of seed. Water, while enroute, is not necessary.

Once home, be sure that all doors and windows in the room are shut, and any open fires or gas flames shielded before the bird is transferred from the traveling box to its cage. The cage door should then be opened, and the box placed alongside. Let the new bird hop from the dark box into the light cage without handling it, if at all possible.

It is best to bring a new bird home during the morning—certainly before noon—so that it has ample time to settle down in its new cage and find a perch before night falls. This is important, because a bird brought in late may spend most of the night fluttering about the cage.

Quite probably, the new bird will not have been in a small cage before, and has taken its food from a hopper or a large open seed pan rather than a seed cup. To train the bird to eat properly, lay a trail of seed from the center of the cage to the seed cup for the first day or so, until it is seen that the bird is taking seed from the container.

DONALD DAULBY

Training a parakeet to land on the finger. Lettuce is being used as a lure. Uncertain as to what is expected of it, the parakeet "buzzes" the finger.

The lure of the lettuce is strong, and here the parakeet backflaps to slow down his air speed.

DONALD DAULBY

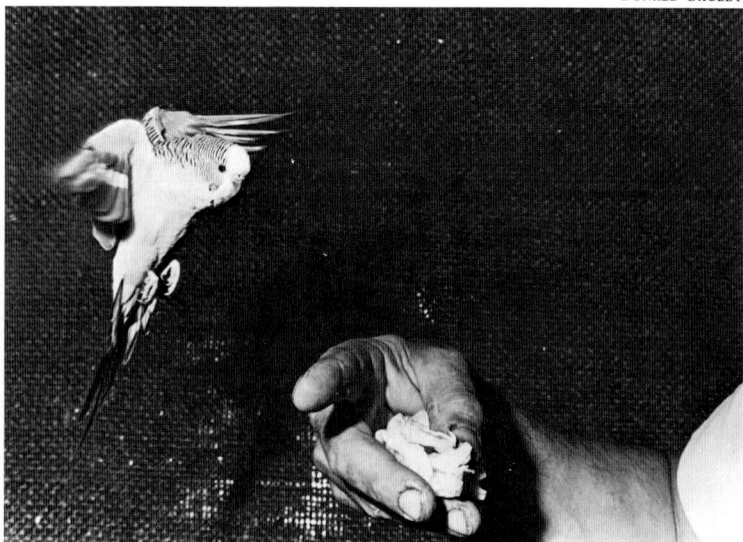

Undercarriage extended, he comes in for a two-point landing.

The first time's always the hardest, after that he has more confidence. If a whistle or other signal is used simultaneously, he will soon learn to respond to the call without the lure.

## Initial Training

The first few days in the new cage are crucial ones, and it is best to accustom the newcomer to its owner right from the first. Your hand in the cage will be accepted by the very young keet as part of the furnishings, particularly if it is moved very slowly. I have known many babies to perch on a finger after fifteen minutes of training, given immediately after they were placed in the cage.

The bird's name—one that is short and clear-cut— should be clearly repeated every time he is fed, given a tidbit and while the cage is being cleaned. It is quite possible that without further coaching he will start to say it himself.

Accustoming the bird to your hand must be done slowly and steadily, and should the first attempts fail, they must be repeated over and over again.

Generally speaking, when the bird realizes that your hand inserted into the cage will not do any harm, he will quiet down and start to investigate. Then the forefinger can be gently moved under the body, pressing against the belly, at the point where the legs join the body, until the bird steps onto the finger. Press gently, but firmly, up and back, until he is forced to step up on your finger. If he flutters wildly about the cage, *don't withdraw your hand*. To do so might lead him to believe that he had "chased" you out, and encourage repetition of this undesirable behavior. Wait until he quiets down, and resume your efforts. Don't leave the cage without some success, no matter how minor.

## Outside the Cage

When he does perch on your finger, maneuver your hand until his breast is pressing against a perch. Transfer him to this while repeating the command "Up!" This should be repeated regularly until he gains enough confidence to allow himself to be slowly taken out of the cage as he sits on the finger. This is a crucial moment, and it should not be attempted until the bird has become completely accustomed to sitting on the hand in the cage. This first journey out should be a short one. Each day the trip can be lengthened.

A lovely picture, showing the confidence which can exist between a bird and a child.

After a careful survey of the room, a parakeet will invariably find a roosting place he prefers and continue to use it from then on. This is a good habit to encourage, as the owner will then always know where first to look for the absentee bird.

A well-trained bird will return quickly to his cage when encouraged by his owner. If he does seem reluctant to leave his perching place, he can usually be persuaded with a Tee-stick or a cane. If the stick is held up near the bird he will hop on; he can then be carried slowly but surely back to his cage.

Every effort should first be made to get the bird to fly back voluntarily. If he must always be caught and handled, it will upset the bird and delay his taming. It's a good idea the first few times to give him his freedom after dark. Should he be reluctant to respond once he senses his freedom, let him perch, turn off all the lights and by quickly flicking a flashlight on and off momentarily, you locate and catch him easily.

Often the budgie will choose a resting place near a mirror or some other shiny object in which he can admire his reflection. Here he will spend a great deal of time muttering and chuckling to himself. Most budgies enjoy toy mirrors (see page 44).

The next step is to encourage the bird to hop from one hand to the other. Keep him moving back and forth. Before long, the bird will—at least this is true of most budgies—climb up the owner's arm and explore other areas of his body.

## Tee-stick Training

Because it is instinctive for a budgerigar to perch on a tree branch, a simulated branch is the logical tool to use in his taming. Some trainers prefer to use their fingers from the very first, and that is the method I have just described, but for those who would rather begin with a stick, here is how to go about it.

A Tee-stick consists of two half-inch dowels joined together to form the letter "T," the handle about two feet long, the cross a few inches wide. It should not be too smooth, or the bird will have trouble staying on it; it should not be so rough that there are splinters.

Now let me digress just a little. Strange as it may seem, a budgie does not recognize the sex of another budgie by its appearance. It is the behavior of the other bird that indicates whether it is male or female, whether it is prepared to challenge, ignore or mate. Aggressive males will face each other directly, whereas a female will turn sideways and bob or bow her head. What does this have to do with training? Very simply this: we make a mistake when we point the stick or a finger directly at the bird and move it towards him. It represents a challenge which usually results in his practically falling over backwards in his haste to avoid this apparently aggressive enemy. The proper way is to bring the stick held horizontally sideways toward the bird, but *very, very* slowly. As a rule, it will not panic him, but as it approaches he may try to fend it off with his beak. Try to move it gently out of his grasp, and persist in directing—but I repeat, ever so slowly—the side of the stick towards the lower part of his body. If he should scramble away, wait until he calms down for a moment and resume your efforts, but do not remove the stick from the cage no matter how panicky he seems. This is one lesson that he *must* learn.

Occasionally, you may find a bird that will respond better to a rear approach, that is the stick is passed around behind his legs and then brought in and pressed forward and upward. The pressure should be firm and steady, so that if he doesn't respond promptly, he is gradually lifted off his perch. If his head starts darting in all directions and he appears nervous, pause for a few minutes until he calms down; otherwise he'll just flee.

## Talk to your Budgie

All through the training sessions, talk soothingly to your budgie. It doesn't matter what you say—he can't understand the words—but the tone of voice, a calm, clear, gentle monotone, will exert a soothing effect and help to familiarize him with you. You can repeat soothingly, "Oh, you are a good boy—yes you are—just step up on it—nobody's going to hurt you," and similar banalities. You can even recite the Declaration of Independence or the Gettysburg Address if you do it soothingly.

Once the bird is up on the stick, reassure him again and move the stick, so now the cage perch is pressing against his leg and he will step back on the perch. Remove your stick, and the first lesson is over. Under no circumstances should you quit without his having stepped on the stick at least once. Regardless of how long it takes, or how tiring it is, this minimum step must be accomplished; otherwise you will find training a difficult procedure later on.

## Climbing the Ladder

After several lessons—by which time he should be stepping promptly on the stick when it is presented to him—prepare two sticks. This time when he steps on the training stick, slowly remove him from the cage. Talk to him quietly while holding him near the cage door and then return him.

nber that the cage is his security—a sort of avian "Linus' blanket"—so be certain there is nothing in the room to distract or disturb him when he is removed. When he becomes accustomed to going in and out the cage door, walk slowly around the room, always talking to him calmly and reassuringly, and return him to the cage. It will help if you tilt the stick upwards and hold your hand fairly high, as a bird always prefers to perch on the highest point. This is when your second stick comes into use. Bring it towards the bird in the same manner as when you started stick training. Coax and persuade him to step up on this; repeat with the first stick and so on, so that in effect, he is climbing a ladder. It will not be long before he steps readily from stick to stick.

If something startles your bird while he is out of the cage, the chances are he will jump off the stick. If he can fly, he will undoubtedly circle the room several times in a panic. If his wings have been clipped, he will flutter to the floor. In

Parakeets are always intrigued by glittering objects and enjoy playing with them.

84

either case, he will be quite upset. Wait calmly until he has settled down, and then approach him slowly with a stick while talking soothingly. Each time he runs or flies away, wait for him to settle down and try again. If circumstances demand that you catch him without delay, toss a towel or a scarf, or even a sweater, over him and pick him up in that. Do not try to catch him with your hands, as a frightened parakeet will bite. The proper way to hold a parakeet is shown on page 87.

**Finger to Finger**

This lesson thoroughly learned, present your finger instead of the stick. Again repeat the step-to-step process, using your hands as steps. By slowly lowering your arm, the budgie will climb up—endeavoring to reach the highest point—and eventually reach your shoulder, from where he may be removed with a stick. If this part of the training is done in front of a mirror, it will be easy to locate the bird when it's time for him to step back on the stick.

**Imprinting**

Those of us who have lived on or visited a farm have seen a hen stalking through the barnyard followed by a group of chicks. Usually they tag along behind in a cluster, as though attached by strings to the mother's body, and if they scatter in the search for food, a gentle "cluck" brings them scurrying back. For the thousands of years that chickens have been domesticated, it has always been taken for granted that chicks follow chickens, ducklings follow ducks, goslings follow geese, cygnets follow swans, and so on, or, as Aesop put it, "birds of a feather flock together."

No one ever stopped to wonder, at least not out loud, why each followed its own kind! Were chicks *born* with the knowledge of their mother's appearance? When they first ran from the nest, why didn't they follow a bull, a sheep or a dog? Finally, definitive studies were undertaken and an answer was found: chicks follow the first moving object they see after hatching. This process is called "imprinting."

Put chicks under a duck, and the newly-hatched chicks will then follow the duck foster-mother. In laboratories, they have even followed wooden blocks and other inanimate objects moved mechanically within the chicks' line of vision. The period when these attachments are formed is very short, varying from a few minutes to a few hours to a few days. This is known as the "critical period" and, in chicks, it is the first few hours after breaking through the shell.

## Thinking Human

No one has made a study of the critical period for imprinting in parakeets, but we do know that a budgie taken from the nest at a very early age and reared with humans seems to fancy himself a human; he will not recognize other parakeets as being of his own kind, and this lack of recognition extends even to mating. It is unusual for a hand-reared keet—that is if he is reared without the company of others of his kind—to successfully mate and raise young. Mating behavior and the rearing patterns are only partially inherited. Their refinement is a matter of evolvement as budgerigars mature in the company of their own kind. Deprived of this cultural experience, they cannot develop the proper behavior.

Of course, the effect is to enhance their value as pets. Parakeets are gregarious flock birds. They don't like to be alone, but enjoy doing things in the company of others. When taken young enough, the budgie accepts humans as his flock and behaves accordingly. Because of this, taming and training a parakeet is seldom a problem. As a rule, they make cheerful and willing performers.

While budgies will live long happy lives all by themselves, they should never be caged alone where they can see and hear, but not physically contact, other keets. The experience is too frustrating and may lead to a physical decline.

## Professional Birds

Many of us have seen trained bird acts in which groups of budgies appear. Offstage, these birds are caged separately and trained individually. Watch closely and you will see that

Above, the wrong way to hold a parakeet.

Below, the proper way.

each bird performs a different trick; they are not taught as a group.

However, this does not mean that a bird which is not hand raised cannot be tamed and trained—far from it. The process involves more time, effort and knowledge, but if you are willing to invest these you can successfully tame and train even the most obstinate parakeet.

So far we have discussed everything in terms of gaining the bird's confidence, familiarizing him with you, and teaching him to enjoy sitting on your finger and shoulder, a process which may take days or weeks or, in the case of an older bird, several months. At this point you will have a thoroughly responsive pet, and if you want to go further with his training it is only a matter of knowledge and an understanding of the principles involved.

**Tricks**

All animals learn by association. The Russian physiologist, Ivan Pavlov, rang a bell each time he fed his dogs. After a number of trials he found that the dogs would salivate at the ringing of the bell in anticipation of the meal. In other words, he had taught them to associate a bell with food. For a reward to be effective it must be closely associated with the action performed, so that the bird can learn that the reward comes as a result of his action.

While parakeets are intelligent birds, there is a limit to their reasoning ability and they are easily distracted. Therefore, we must select some method of directing their attention to the proper performance immediately when it is done. For this purpose, professional trainers have found a small cricket or snapper most suitable. This is the children's toy which makes a click, something like a castanet, when the metal tongue is pressed. A suitable reward is also required, and for parakeets the most effective is millet spray.

**Withholding Food**

While food is normally kept in front of a parakeet at all times, in preparation for the training remove all food several hours earlier. Once your bird is accustomed to being handled, try hand feeding him. Start by offering him millet with one hand, while holding the snapper in the other. As he takes the millet, click the snapper. Each time you give him a treat, snap the cricket. It will not take too long before he will associate the sound of the cricket with the treat.

As to what tricks to teach, much depends on the nature of the bird himself. I have always found it is best to let "games" develop naturally. One of my budgies got tremendous enjoyment from picking up small coins on a table, and then taking them to the edge and dropping them to the floor. As soon as one coin was dropped, he went after another one, and that went over too, until all the coins were on the floor. Then he would hop down to the floor himself and turn all the coins over. When he tired of this he would fly up and sit on my shoulder and murmur sweet nothings in my ear, waiting for me to replace the coins on the table. I don't know who got tired of this game first, but it was certainly good exercise for us both.

**Bathing Beauties**

Some budgies like to swim, which is strange, since most of them balk even at taking a bath. If you can tempt yours to try the water, you'll have no end of fun watching him show off.

Start out with a small clear glass bowl, not a ceramic one. Fill it with water. Do not force the bird in, but let him play around the bowl until he decides to investigate. It may take several days. After a few swims, you can give him a bigger "tank"—a goldfish bowl or an aquarium.

It is best to put in a wood block, two by about three inches long, with a cord wrapped around one end to give him a foothold to climb up when he gets tired. He will shake himself, and soon learn to paddle this "raft" around like a child pedaling a scooter. Of course, you will never leave him alone in the tank; always keep an eye on him when he is in bathing. *Never, never, never* leave his "bathtub" full of water when you are not there, unless it has an absolutely budgie-proof covering. The same goes for the tropical fish tank, as well

Budgerigars are great company for invalids and shut-ins. They require very little attention and are a constant source of interest and amusement.

HARRY LACEY

as other similar containers of water, including open toilet bowls. Many a budgie has been unable to negotiate the smooth sides after jumping in for a bath, and with his feathers wet he can't fly—a tragic end.

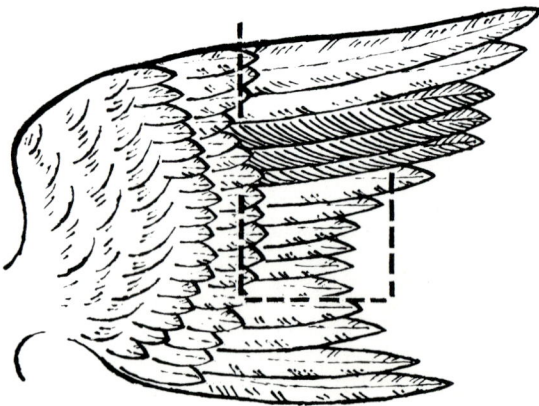

MICHAEL YOUENS

Some keepers prefer to clip their bird's wings during the training period. The broken lines show which feathers should be cut away on both wings.

## Wing Clipping

There is diversity of opinion about clipping a pet budgie's wings to prevent its flying before it is really tame. I have tried both clipping and non-clipping, and I am still not sure which is best. Here again, the temperament of the individual bird is the controlling factor.

I would suggest that you try hand taming without clipping, unless your pet proves recalcitrant, and then you have little choice.

If you do decide to clip, clip both wings by using sharp scissors and cutting all the flight feathers about half an inch from the edge of the wing bone, leaving the three last long feathers intact. See the drawing on page 90. Cutting feathers does not hurt the bird in any way, and the cut feathers will drop out and be replaced by new ones at the first molt. They will then have to be cut again if the bird has not been fully tamed.

## Children and Parakeets

Which is the source of greater delight, the child for the parakeet, or the parakeet for the child? Parakeets are affectionate, eager to play and—because of their ability to talk and learn tricks—a never-ending source of entertainment.

On the practical side, a parakeet is a fine educational pet. Breeding parakeets is a simple and understandable way to teach a child the "facts of life" with no elaborate lectures necessary. Simply provide the birds with a nest box and let what happens happen. You can answer the questions the child asks with as much or little detail as will satisfy his curiosity.

Too, the older child can help to feed and care for the pet, and this will provide invaluable lessons with regard to respect for life and living things, the need for cleanliness of person, and so on. The beauty of it is that it is all so effortless and natural.

So to answer the opening question: Perhaps it is the adult, observing both the child *and* parakeet, who is most delighted!

What a fine fellow I am!

# VII   Teaching your Budgie to Talk

If you have followed the suggestions given in the chapter on Training, your pet is now ready for this next step.

As I have already pointed out, some parakeets are more skilful at talking than others. Both male and female will learn to talk if they are hand raised from the nest, and tamed when very young; but there is a great deal of difference in the learning ability of the individual. However, with perseverence, almost any parakeet, even an older one, can be taught to mimic to some degree.

Before a bird will begin to talk, he must feel comfortable and relaxed in the presence of his trainer; nor should he ever be frightened by other pets, boisterous children or sudden noises and abrupt movements. If a bird becomes timid and fearful in the beginning, weeks of hard work will be needed to regain his lost confidence. This is why a new arrival should be placed where he can observe people, and yet be far enough away not to be alarmed by the normal bustle of the household.

If a parakeet is never let out of his cage, just fed and watered, but ignored the rest of the day, one cannot expect him to talk. Attention and kindness—so that the bird will come to love and trust you—are the essential ingredients.

## Intelligence

Always remember that a talking bird is a mimic; he does not reason. He repeats by rote words and sentences he has been taught, or ones that he has overheard. What sometimes appears to be thinking, as when a bird answers a question, is simply a matter of word association, while a good morning greeting or a goodnight farewell, appropriately delivered, are merely time associations.

## Sex

In my opinion, the sex of the bird has no bearing whatsoever on his ability to imitate. In a great many cases, an owner is not even aware of the sex of his new pet. As already pointed out, it is only when the budgerigar is older that the male can be distinguished from the female by the color of his cere.

As to the sex of the trainer, this is a different matter. All are agreed that women and children make the best speech teachers. There is something in their voices that has a more soothing effect on budgies, and the pitch and tone are closer to the bird's own, and therefore easier to imitate.

## Under Cover

Many trainers believe that a bird learns to talk more quickly if the cage is covered during the training session. I personally have found no evidence for this. I feel that the bird likes to see, as well as hear, his trainer. However, there are many who disagree with me, and if you should discover that your bird does learn faster when covered, or when you remain out of sight, by all means use this method. Sometimes just

Please repeat after me. . . .

LOUISE VAN DER MEID

covering the back and two sides of the cage increases the bird's concentration.

## Attention

Particularly in the beginning, when the budgie is still learning, his attention should be completely concentrated on the trainer, so no toys or other distractions like mirrors should be left in the cage. Do not try to teach two birds at a time, or even keep them both in the same room during training sessions. They will imitate each other, not you.

## Improprieties

While it sometimes seems like fun to teach vulgar words and oaths, one should always bear in mind that the bird may utter them at an inappropriate moment. Talking birds seem to pick up "swear words" quite readily; this is probably because such expressions are sharp and distinct, and usually uttered with explosive force.

## A "Secret" Method

Here is a summary of what a very accomplished bird trainer told me about her method. To begin with, she pointed out, we must remember that teaching parakeets to talk only *seems* to be a slow process. We should realize that it takes a child nearly two years before he does much talking. Why be impatient with a bird?

Many people have asked her about her method, thinking perhaps she had found some great secret. "The secret," she insists, "is patience and perseverance—and nothing else!"

She believes that birds learn best between seven and nine o'clock in the morning, and between seven and nine in the evening, and that they also talk more during these two periods. She thinks the bird learns faster if he does not watch you during the lesson, that he pays closer attention if you remain just out of his sight range.

She then says clearly whatever word or phrase she wishes the bird to learn, and always pauses between each repetition for it to sink in. She never utters another expression during the entire period. She is particularly careful not to speak to a dog or cat, or to any person who might be in the house. She repeats the chosen phrase for at least a quarter of an hour, morning and evening. She then leaves the bird alone, without even a word of endearment or parting, to think over what he has just heard. Otherwise, she points out, it is quite possible that the extraneous interjections may be jumbled into the expression you are trying to teach.

Supplement the regular training sessions by using the same word or phrase whenever you are in the room with the parakeet, and especially when you greet him in the morning and after you have turned out the light at night.

If a new parakeet does not begin to talk after a reasonable time, change your method; try training him in a darkened room twice each day for a half hour. It is better to sit where the parakeet can hear, but not see you. Many trainers have reported that, with their patience exhausted, they had given up regular training, only to overhear the bird some time later uttering clearly the word or phrase that they had tried for so long to teach. Usually when a bird starts to pick up speech, he will sit hunched up for minutes at a time mumbling and muttering under his breath until he has perfected the word or phrase.

It goes without saying that a bird should never be punished for stubbornly refusing to repeat the word or phrase you are trying to teach him. Punishment will only make things worse.

Now it's your turn to talk!

## Word and Time Association

Perhaps you would like to have your bird show off by answering questions. "Who's the greatest?" perhaps, to have the parakeet reply, "I am!" Start by teaching the answer first; in this case, "I am!" He will, of course, eventually learn to repeat both question and answer, sometimes together, sometimes interchangeably, but this too can be amusing.

Parakeets appear to have a great sense of time and occasion. When and where you teach the desired expression has a great bearing on its time of repetition. A "Good morning" taught in the morning will almost always be uttered only in the morning, and a "Good night" taught in the evening will be repeated only then. If the bird learns the name of a food as it is being fed, he will be inclined to repeat that name only when he sees the food. Budgies quickly learn the names of the members of the family, and of other pets, and almost always use them correctly.

While I am of the opinion that a parakeet must first be hand tamed before he will begin to speak, there are those who believe that taming and talk-training can go hand in hand. They remove all food and water from the cage in the afternoon (or offer none at all except during the training session) and then the next morning feed and water the new arrival entirely by hand, and as they do so they utter the word or phrase they want the bird to learn.

For example, they say "Good morning" and then present a tasty seed or nut, and again more food with a "Good morning" and so on. The adherents to this "reward" theory believe that by identifying the phrase with the food, the word becomes a pleasing sound, one that the bird welcomes. Then låter on, when the bird is alone, he will have been conditioned into uttering the expression to attract attention —and, of course, if he does so, he should be rewarded immediately with food and soothing compliments.

Once the bird repeats the phrase, he should, of course, never be rewarded until after the phrase has been uttered. Then lessons on a new phrase can begin.

As the bird becomes more and more tame, he will become more and more attached to his trainer, and the reward will then be the trainer's mere presence. The bird will talk to bring the trainer to him, remain silent while the trainer is present and resume talking if the trainer starts to leave.

Many owners never realize their pet's full talking potential. When their bird has learned a few words or phrases, they abandon all further training. This is a mistake. The most difficult teaching period is the one before the bird utters his first word. After that it is all clear sailing, but still a certain amount of concentrated effort is required and the phrases that have been learned should constantly be reviewed.

### Recordings

There are on the market a number of phonograph records that can be used for teaching a parakeet to talk. If you do not

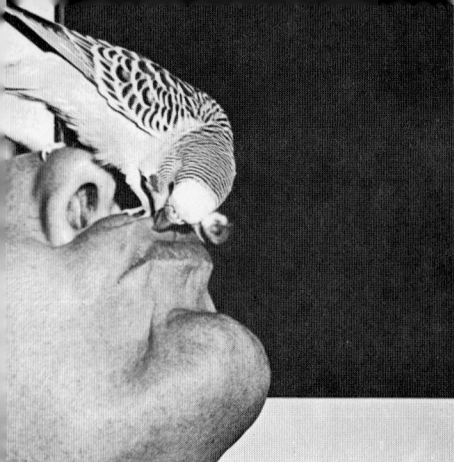

Is this where all those strange sounds come from?

This requires a little investigation!

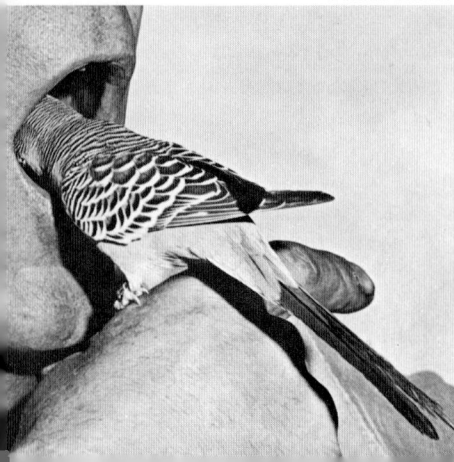

Say ah—and keep saying it! Love and confidence; the little budgie trusts his master completely.

have the time or patience to teach the bird yourself, these records can be very helpful. But perhaps an even better idea, if you have a tape-recorder, is to tape one of your own training sessions and then repeatedly play it back to the bird while you go about your household duties, because a parakeet mimics not just the word, but also the tone of voice and the inflection. It is flattering to hear your own voice repeated.

Mimicry is not just limited to words; a parakeet will sing or whistle a tune, do bird calls, bark like a dog or meow like a cat—any noise which he hears often enough to be impressed on his memory will be repeated eventually, even the sound of inanimate objects like the car horn, a door slamming or a motor. A "wolf-whistle" is something which all parakeets pick up quite readily, often even before learning to talk.

Some people prefer to confine a bird to its cage during the speech training session.

Finger-tame pets seldom make good breeders.

# VIII   Breeding

Quite frequently a healthy female budgerigar kept by her-self as a pet will present her owner with a clutch of eggs, and I am often asked what to do in such cases, as unwanted eggs often cause concern to an owner unfamiliar with the ways of birds. Let me hasten to say that egg-laying is a natural function that does not harm a hen; it is the rearing of fast-growing chicks that can sap the mother's energy. When a pet does lay a clutch of eggs—which, of course, will be infertile—it is best to leave a couple of them with her, so that she can continue to sit on them if she desires. This will prolong the time between unwanted clutches and keep her happy.

Sometimes one owner has a hen and his friend a cock, and they decide to let their birds "get married" and divide the young ones that result from the union. This, of course, is not a bad idea, provided that, as frequently happens, one or both doesn't think of itself as a human rather than as a budgie. In that case, it will be unable to relate to its partner and cannot function as a breeder. If nature should assert itself, both families will have the fun of a breeding pair, watching the eggs and the baby budgies develop. It should be realized, however, that once the birds have gotten to know each other, they almost invariably lose their extreme tameness and become unsuitable as pets.

## Two in a Cage

In nature, parakeets—like most parrot-type birds—nest in the hollows of limbs or tree trunks. If your pet should lay her

One type of commercially available nest box. The concave block (removable for cleaning) prevents the eggs from rolling. The inner, glass panel is to keep the birds from escaping when the sliding door is opened for observation.

eggs on the gravel tray, the chances of her successfully incubating them and then raising the young are practically nil. So if you should decide to encourage the propagation of the species, you must provide your pair with a nest box, several types of which are illustrated in this book. There is no one superior type; all have proven successful.

While breeding in the average home cage is less than desirable, still it is an exciting experience, and especially for children it is a memorable one.

Because most home cages are too small to contain the nest box, it is usually hung or mounted on the outside of the cage with the entrance hole (pophole) in line with and flush against the open cage doorway. The perch should protrude through the box so that it extends both inside and outside the box. Of course this makes it impossible for you to gain access to the cage through the doorway without removing the nest box, but most cages are arranged so that the food and water dishes can be serviced from the sides.

Most breeders place a handful of coarse sawdust in the box, but some prefer to leave it bare, and depend on the concave nest block to keep the eggs from scattering.

Actual mating is preceded and accompanied by a great deal of billing and mutual preening, during the course of which the male feeds the female by regurgitation. Her cere turns dark brown and appears wrinkled. His cere is plump and bright blue; his eyes sparkle and the pupils expand and contract rapidly.

The mating act is accomplished by the male mounting the female; while balancing himself on her with fluttering wings, he swings his tail under hers, so as to contact her cloaca with his, at which time the sperm is transferred. Unless this takes place, eggs when laid will be infertile.

Egglaying starts about eight days after mating, with one laid every other day. There can be up to eight eggs in a clutch, but it is best to keep only four or five.

Incubation takes about eighteen days, with an egg hatching every other day after that. This is important, because if they all hatched at the same time, the parents would be unable to provide enough of the first food.

Stimulated by the brooding, both parents' crops secrete

Fourteen to sixteen days old, and
the feathers are just coming in.

a thick milky substance composed primarily of fat and
protein. The parent takes the hatchling's beak into its own,
and forcibly regurgitates this food, in effect pumping it
down into the baby. As the babies grow, this gradually dries
up and seed which the parent has eaten replaces it. The babies
are fed this way until they leave the nest.

Ample food and water must be provided during the breeding as well as extra portions of soft foods. (See Feeding.)

Usually a second round of eggs is laid before all the first
hatchlings are out. If this happens, the male will take over
the chore of feeding the older group, while the female
incubates the new.

A pair of parakeets should not be allowed more than two
nests a year. Breeding is terminated simply by removing
the nest box. (For additional information, see the chapter
on Advanced Breeding.)

**Colony Breeding**

After keeping a pet for some time, the owner may get the
urge to breed budgerigars, first as a hobby, and then, perhaps
later, for profit. A great deal of fun and excitement can be
had from maintaining a small aviary of various colored
budgerigars, and breeding them on the "colony" system.

A very successful commercial breeder designed this nest box. The extra wooden block is to give the hen something to chew on; the large front door opens downwards to avoid pinching or trapping a foot or toe; the concave block is set slightly back for the same reason and to one side so the hen doesn't drop on her eggs or young; youngsters which are being bothered by adults can escape them by slipping under the "bench."

HARRY LACEY

This means the breeding together in one enclosure of several pairs of budgerigars, as opposed to breeding selected pairs in individual cages.

In their wild state, budgerigars are gregarious and breed in large colonies, so the average keeper of budgerigars who does not want to exhibit his birds or breed special colors will find colony breeding his answer.

The prospective breeder can, of course, start with only one pair of birds. While it is often said that a single pair kept on its own will not breed, I have not found this true. Most single pairs breed freely and well.

Budgerigars are adaptable birds that can be housed for breeding purposes in a great variety of structures. If only a single pair is used at the start, then a large box-type cage is best. This should be of ample dimensions, at least 3 feet long, 18 inches high and 18 inches deep, to give the birds plenty of flight room; if possible, these dimensions should be even larger. Such a cage can be situated in an outbuilding, patio, or, if suitably shielded from the weather, outside in the garden—in fact, almost any place the owner has space to spare.

## Outdoor Flights

Budgies breed best in the open where they can get fresh

air and natural sunlight. This is undoubtedly a throwback to their feral state. Australian naturalists have reported dozens of budgerigar nests in the same hollow limb. No artificial heat is necessary unless the temperature drops to below freezing; then the birds must be shut into a dry, draftproof shelter which should be heated to no more than 40°F. Overheating can produce an artificial breeding condition, which is bad for the birds.

An outdoor aviary can be as functional or as elaborate as the owner wishes. How to plan and construct one is discussed in Chapter IV.

Successful colony breeding demands that the breeding pairs not be overcrowded. In fact, it is better to under-populate an aviary than it is to try and squeeze in a few extra birds. Nor is it a good idea to have an "extra lady" in the flight; this can only be an invitation to trouble. Hens are jealous and spiteful, and one too many in a colony is bound to incite quarrels. On the other hand, an "extra man" is as welcome here as he is at a dinner party, because his presence will spur the other males to get on with their courting.

As I have said, in their natural state, budgerigars breed in hollow branches and rotting logs. In captivity they are just as happy with wooden nest boxes. I discuss these at length in Chapter IX.

Special care must be taken when positioning these boxes to minimize squabbling. All the boxes should be hung as high as possible, at *exactly* the same height, with their pop-holes facing the brightest part of the aviary. When the birds are first paired, there should be two boxes available for each couple, so they can have a choice of boxes; this, too, will help to reduce squabbling. When the pairs have mated, the unused boxes can be removed. If one particular pair of birds, or even just one hen, is troublesome to the others, isolate them.

## Perches

Perches, both in the shelter and the flight, should be attached firmly. Nor should they be too smooth. As I have said, branches with the bark left on make the best perches. When perches are loose or smooth, the budgerigars often fail to connect when mating, because they cannot get a firm grip. Often breeders have discarded a hen thinking she was sterile when the trouble lay in the fact she had never been properly impregnated.

## Color Choice

The prospective breeder is often faced with the problem of which colors to breed. Before this can definitely be decided, it is advisable to have some idea of the many beautiful shades that are available, and how they reproduce when bred together. (See Chapters XII and XIII.)

With the colony system there is, of course, no guarantee that cross pairing will not take place even though the birds may have chosen their mates before being placed in the aviary. While parakeets are monogamous, a certain amount of infidelity does occur.

If the novice breeder wants a good selection of prettily colored young ones, I suggest that each cock bird be one of the following colors: Sky Blue, White Cobalt, Opaline Sky

HORST MÜLLER

Nearly ready to leave the nest box.

Blue and Yellow-face Cobalt; their mates can be Light Green, Albino, Cinnamon Sky Blue and Graywing Cobalt. This makes four pairs, and no matter how they cross-mate, the majority of the young will belong to the Blue-colored group. If, for instance, the White Cobalt pairs with the pure Graywing Cobalt they will have all Graywing-colored young—but of three different shades, for example, Graywing Sky Blue, Graywing Cobalt and Graywing Mauve. If the Opaline Sky Blue cock selects as his mate the Albino (Sky Blue) hen, they will give normally-colored Sky Blue cocks and Opaline Sky Blue hens, and should the Yellow-face Cobalt cock pair with the Cinnamon Sky Blue hen, the resulting young will be Sky Blues, Cobalts, Yellow-face Sky Blues and Yellow-face Cobalts.

From this it will be seen that these birds can produce many more colors than there were originally, and that many of the young will carry hidden in their genetic makeup the possibility of breeding even other colors. That is just a small suggestion of what can be done to produce many lovely shades. I must point out here that if the breeder wants attractive colors, the birds known as Grays and Gray Greens should not be included in the colony.

If the novice breeder prefers to produce young cocks to train as talking pets, and wants to be able to identify them at an early age, he can plan certain matings which will produce chicks with an identifying color. These sex-linked varieties are the Opalines, the Cinnamons and the Albinos (Lutinos).

If, for instance, only Opaline cocks are included in the colony along with non-Opaline hens, the resulting young will all be Opaline *hens* and non-Opaline *cocks*. The breeder will then know that every chick that is not an Opaline must be male. It is as simple as that! The working of the sex-linked character is fully explained in Chapter XIII.

Having chosen the breeding pairs and installed them in their aviary, along with correctly positioned nest boxes, rich food, water and all the other accouterments, the breeder must then wait for the eggs to start appearing. If the birds are healthy—and they should be if they are expected to breed—the hens should start to lay within two weeks, one egg appearing every other day. Allow eight days from fertilization to egg laying. The normal clutch is from five or six up to eight eggs, but most breeders take away all but four eggs, distributing the excess to nests that have less than four. However, the eggs in these other nests must have been laid at approximately the same time. The incubation period is approximately 18 days.

What must be watched in colony breeding is that the fledglings are not allowed to remain in the common aviary too long. They mature quickly, and are likely to begin breeding when they are three or four months old; no cock should be allowed to mate until he is at least ten months old, and no hen until a year old.

The best breeding season in the northern hemisphere is from March 1 to September 30.

## Second Clutch

Budgerigars are usually allowed no more than two clutches a year, although they themselves will be quite willing to go on indefinitely. Unlimited breeding can only result in poor quality youngsters, and reduce the parents' vigor. However, if the first or second nests are failures, with no chicks hatched, a third clutch can be allowed since, as I have said, it is the raising of the chicks that causes the strain on the parents.

As I said earlier, the hen will sometimes start to lay her second clutch even before the last chicks of the first clutch have left the nest, and this should be avoided if at all possible.

To the experienced eye, budgies have an individual character almost as soon as they are hatched. The golden glow of the quills and the red eye indicate that the baby on the right is a Lutino.

# IX   Advanced Breeding

Many beginners think that all they have to do is put a male and female budgerigar together in a cage with seed, water and grit, and give them a nest box; that about ten days later there will be an egg in the box and another one every other day after that; that in 19 days the first egg will hatch, and within eight days they will have a boxful of nestlings; that a month later, four magnificent budgies will be flying around the cage, and they will have quadrupled their investment. If it were only as easy as all that!

I have already pointed out that there are two methods of breeding budgerigars: Controlled breeding and Colony breeding; and as I said in the chapter on Aviaries, the colony method is more or less a hit-and-miss system, with the birds pairing and breeding at will. The serious breeder does not even consider this method because he wants full genetic control. It is not entirely a hit-and-miss method, however, or if it is, it doesn't matter when all the birds are of the same color and color heritage, or you are breeding for the pet market—in fact, it might be better to get your first breeding experience this way. But if you intend to breed breeders or exhibition birds, you will have to use strict control.

This means that each pair, after it has been carefully selected (see page 118), is housed by itself, in a separate flighted "apartment" or compartment, as they are commonly called. These apartments, in turn, are combined in blocks of four to twelve to form an apartment house or "control aviary." The picture on page 52 shows structures of this type.

Each compartment, of course, is completely furnished with its own seed, water and gravel vessels. Seed hoppers and water reservoirs are useful if the birds cannot be given personal attention every day; they are of special value when you want to take a day off. I have tried both open vessels and seed hoppers, and although personally I prefer the open vessels, I have found the automatic hoppers and drinkers dependable and easy to handle.

## Nest Boxes

As there is only one pair of birds to a cage or compartment, only a single nest box is needed for each couple. I say this, even though it sounds obvious, because I advised that in colony breeding two nest boxes be allotted to each couple.

I fix all my boxes at the same height, with the pophole facing the brightest part of the shelter. These boxes should be firmly attached so that they do not wobble when the birds go in and out. I have known many nests to be spoiled because the owner neglected to make sure that all the boxes were firmly secured before the hens started to lay.

There are on the market many different types of budgerigar nest boxes, as you will see from pictures in these chapters. The sizes vary, as does the location of the popholes and inspection doors, but they all have a common factor—a removable concave block in the bottom.

The nest box that I have found the most satisfactory is nine inches long, five inches wide, and six inches high, with an inspection door at the side and the pophole and perch in front. The removable bottoms are made of one-inch board, with the actual hollow being some three quarter-inches deep in the center and oval in shape. The boxes themselves are made of half-inch pine and are sturdily constructed to last many years, even under the onslaught of nesting budgerigar hens. It is advantageous to use such thick wood because it helps to keep eggs from drying up, and at the same time, insulates parents and eggs against sudden temperature changes. As the budgerigar does not build a nest in the accepted sense of the word, it is not necessary to provide any nesting material.

I have found that creosote used to paint nesting boxes acts as a deterrent to lice and, in particular, the troublesome Red Mite. Not only do I paint the outside of the boxes, I paint the inside bottom, and the bottom and side of the nest blocks. After the breeding season, I thoroughly wash all of the nest boxes with a strong disinfectant, and when they are dry, give them a new coat of creosote, which I allow to dry thoroughly before returning them to storage in plastic bags for use the following spring.

While on the subject of nest boxes, I recall the first time I used them. Up to that time I had used coconut husks. Information about budgerigar breeding was scarce, and I heard about the then-new nesting boxes in a roundabout way. I thought them an excellent idea, and made myself a half a dozen about nine inches square, with a pophole and lid. My budgies took to them at once, and proceeded to produce clutches of eggs. Much to my horror, although the eggs were fertile, not one of them hatched, and this went on for two rounds. Then one day at a bird club meeting, I chanced to encounter a much more experienced fancier, and he told me where I had gone wrong: my boxes had a plain flat bottom and consequently the eggs rolled all over the bottom whenever the hen moved; therefore, no chicks! As soon as I fitted concave bottoms, everything went smoothly. Since that time I have always used boxes of my own making.

Make sure that your nest boxes have no gaps in the joints, and that the doors fit snugly. It is a good idea to have replaceable concave blocks to make cleaning easier. Always see that the nest box gives the birds a sense of security. Make sure that the pophole is large enough for them to go in and out easily, and that they can reach it from the nest when they're inside; if not, it is possible for them to become trapped and

This Opaline Sky Blue cock and Cinnamon Green hen produced three young in the first nest, all Blue colors. This shows that the hen is split to Blue, but in future nests, Green colors will probably be produced.

starve. The outside perch should extend two inches into the box.

Some breeders have successfully used nest boxes constructed from heavy cardboard, but with the usual wood concave block for the nest. Such boxes are, of course, discarded after each use.

## Pen Method

In addition to individual control flights, some breeders use the control pen method of breeding, and this is useful when space is limited or when weather conditions are unsuitable. I have used control pens myself for many years, with excellent results.

These pens are, in fact, the same in construction as the shelter sections of controlled flighted aviaries, minus the flights. The only difference is that I use round or oval perches that can be bought at pet supply stores in place of natural wood perches. This is my own idea; if the breeder prefers natural wood perches, they can be used.

The only advantage that pen breeding has over cage breeding is that it provides the breeding birds with more space in which to exercise, and this keeps them in top condition for longer periods.

## Cage Method

A high percentage of the control-bred budgerigars is produced in cages. For those breeders who have limited outdoor space or live in large cities, cage breeding is the only answer. Cages can be purchased or made in sizes to fit each individual breeder's birdroom, and his own special ideas can be incorporated into the scheme.

In my firm opinion, the minimum size of these breeding cages should be no less than some 35 inches long, 12 inches deep and 14 inches high. They should not be any smaller than this, and if they can be larger, so much the better. Such cages will allow the breeding pairs a reasonable amount of space in which to move freely. If cages are too cramped, there is always the possibility of the birds acquiring bad habits, such as feather plucking or egg eating, out of sheer boredom.

Breeding cages can be constructed of lumber, hardboard, plywood or a mixture of all three, and the fronts can be ordinary small mesh wire netting, welded mesh netting or commercially made cage fronts which can be purchased separately.

If sand trays are to be used on cage bottoms, they can be drawers of the same material as the cages, although rustproof metal is preferred. Baking trays and their like can be utilized. Removable sand trays make cage cleaning simpler and, of course, are more sanitary.

Whenever possible the cages should be built in units with each row connected by sliding partitions. These partitions should be made of an opaque material and so well fitted that each cage can be fully screened from its neighbors during the breeding season.

By doing this, the breeder can, by removing the partitions, make three or four cages into one long flight cage for the use of youngsters and adults during the non-breeding periods. As I have already stressed, flying exercise is most important if cage stock is to be maintained in vigorous health.

When not needed for breeding purposes, the individual sections can be used as stock or training cages for exhibition birds. When the cages are used for this purpose, the nesting boxes should be removed.

For decorating the interiors of home-built cages I find that white gloss enamel is most satisfactory. Be sure that there is no lead or other toxic material in the formula. Gloss enamel dries quickly and hard, and if any is eaten it does no harm. The same paint can be used on the outside or, if preferred, a color of your choice can be used. The wirework can be painted or not, as you wish. Black helps to make it less visible.

I myself use white emulsion paint for both inside and out,

An adult hen with only one chick. The maximum size to which chicks can grow is fixed at the time of fertilization, so the idea that one always produces larger birds by keeping only one or two chicks in each nest is not necessarily correct. However, if there are more than four babies in the nest, there is a possibility that they will not all develop to their fullest potential.

HARRY LACEY

as I find it easy to apply, inexpensive, and above all, safe for the birds. I cannot stress too strongly the danger to parakeets of toxic paints and lead. This is also true of giving them chunks of old plaster. While the plaster itself is good for them, there is always the danger that it has been painted with a lead paint. Children, too, have been poisoned this way.

All painted surfaces must be thoroughly dried before the birds are put into the cages; if the paint gets on their feathers it can spoil their looks for a long time.

## Hanging Nest Boxes

There is a difference of opinion as to whether nest boxes should be hung inside the cage, or attached outside with the pophole and its perch opening into the cage. I always hang mine inside since I have observed that budgies have more fun and are inclined to nest more quickly if they can climb all over their boxes. This is my personal opinion; there are many breeders who prefer the outside type, since they are easier to inspect. However, this is a matter which breeders must decide for themselves, taking into consideration space and the particular nesting behavior of their birds.

## Stock

Once the breeding quarters are built and equipped, the breeder must then think about obtaining the necessary breeding stock. For successful results, it is important to install the birds in their new quarters some time before they are expected to breed. This will enable them to get fully acquainted with their new surroundings. If stock birds are not given this settling-in period, they may be reluctant to start breeding and, in extreme cases, have been known to miss a complete season.

It is always best to get stock from a reliable breeder. Choose birds that are wearing the breeder's closed ring bands, dated for the year of breeding. The color and exhibition breeder should endeavor to get the full pedigrees of all the birds he purchases (as well as keeping records on those he breeds himself) right from the start. I find that young stock

Just out of the egg.

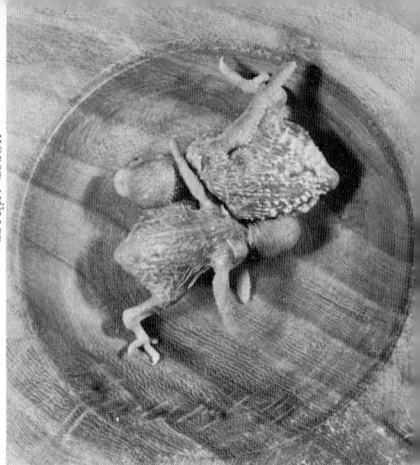

Four and six days old.

HORST MÜLLER

The oldest chick is about two weeks old.

▲ HORST MÜLLER

▲ HARRY LACEY

Eight and ten days old.

Various stages of growth in the same nest; the oldest is about three weeks.

Three and a half weeks old, quite alert and anxious to be fed.

HARRY LACEY

Fully feathered at five weeks old, the youngsters scramble out of the nest when disturbed. The egg at the bottom is the start of a new clutch.

settle down in new surroundings far more readily than older birds that have already been bred. The initial stock should be limited—I'd say no more than five or six pairs—until the new breeder has gained some knowledge of the general management of budgerigars and become more familiar with their ways.

As my readers will learn from reading Chapter XII, colors and varieties of budgerigars are legion, and it is essential that consideration be given to the color variety of the first stock birds. If this is not done, a good sound start cannot be made as the breeder will have too many "bits and pieces"

A proud hen with a fine nest of chicks.

HARRY LACEY

for openers. I suggest that before any birds are actually purchased, the potential breeder see as many differently colored budgies as possible, either by visiting established aviaries or cage bird exhibitions. He will then be able to make a wise choice for color, and having done so, proceed to buy the right birds with the right genetic strain.

I must point out that the color of budgerigars has no bearing on their breeding capabilities; birds of any color can be poor or good breeders. However, different strains and families can each have their own special breeding traits which can, of course, affect their productivity.

I urge all new breeders not to try and mate up all their stock on a given date. It is much more satisfactory to mate the birds as they come into condition, even though it may mean waiting for some weeks before the complete stud is in the breeding cages.

**Planned Matings**

Having settled the birds in their new home (males separated

from females) well before the start of the breeding season, the breeder can then begin to match them up on paper and work out his expected percentages. The simplified tables included in Chapter XIII will help with this. The next step is to actually choose the pairs.

For this there are two approaches, by visual observation and by pedigree. When planning your matings, do not "average" your birds; that is, do not match a run-of-the-mill cock with a near-perfect hen, or vice versa. All that can be expected from such a mating will be average offspring.

Two birds with the same fault, even if it is a minor fault, should not be mated. Nor should opposites—good head to poor head, for instance. You cannot, of course, expect a hen to have the same type of head as a cock; there is a physical difference between the sexes. Too, some colors and varieties possess individual and characteristic type differences according to sex.

What you should do is choose your very best cock for your very best hen; your second best cock for your second best hen, and so on down the line—but not *too* far down. You would not, of course, want to mate pairs that could be described as poor, or even fair. Sometimes, by chance, two birds unsuited visually do give birth to a very good specimen, but the odds are that the offspring of such a specimen, when mated, will produce inferior birds.

## Pedigree Breeding

This, the mating of related birds, is the only method that can give you even a reasonable amount of genetic control. It is also known as linebreeding or inbreeding. In genetics, inbreeding usually refers to the mating of close relatives—parent to child, brother to sister—while linebreeding is the term used for more distant relationships.

Obviously, with stock whose ancestry is unknown—and this should be true for only your first season—you will have to resort to visual pairings unless you have purposely purchased matched pairs, birds guaranteed to be linebred.

If the type is good, the closer the relationship of the birds, the better, and then not too much careful planning will be needed since mating closely related birds sends the odds up in your favor, although I know of no sure-fire system that automatically produces top quality birds.

These linebred birds can be mated so safely—that is if they match visually—because both members are carrying the same genetic factors for the good points and not the same factors for the faults.

It was once believed that inbreeding is harmful, but unless some measure of linebreeding is practiced the genes carrying the wanted characteristics can become so dispersed in the general budgerigar population as to render most unlikely the possibility that a pair, both possessing the same wanted genes, will ever meet and mate by chance. This is why mutations seldom become established in the wild.

I hope by now I have made it clear that mating birds of the same bloodline increases the probability of the desired mating results being achieved.

## Second Generation

At the end of your first breeding season, after your fledglings have gone through their first molt and you can distinguish their sexes and get some idea of their visual types, separate the males from the females and single out the best male. Compare him with his father. If he is good, set him aside until the next breeding season to be mated with his mother. This, known as backcrossing, will establish a strain based on the hen.

Do the same with the best fledgling hen. Breed her back to her father. This will establish a bloodline based on the male.

Do the same with the second generation, backcrossing the birds with their parents, and so on. You can also cross brothers and sisters. By the end of the third season you will have established two strong bloodlines, one descending from the first cock, one from the first hen.

If faults begin to appear consistently, new and unrelated birds will, from time to time, have to be introduced into the bloodlines.

You will, of course, band all these birds (see page 130) and

The bird on the left is a Banded type of Australian Pied Blue with the band slightly broken in the center. She has the characteristic clear flights and tail, but is lacking in type and stance. She should be mated to a bold Normal Sky Blue cock for best results. The Dominant Australian Pied Green has more substance, but not enough color either in the band or in the broken patches on the chest. A good mate for her would be a substantially built Light Green or Sky Blue.

keep a careful record so that there can be no confusion when mating time comes around.

## Mating

Before I actually pair a cock with a hen I always put them in small cages placed side by side (old show cages are excellent for this) to see if my paper selection is correct. Only when I have satisfied myself that the pair is well matched and ready to breed do I put the birds together in a large breeding cage.

I do not, however, give them their nest box at once. I leave them on their own the first few days and watch them to make sure they are compatible. If all goes well, and the birds take to each other readily, the boxes can be installed a few days later.

There is another reason for not giving the pairs their nest boxes right away. I have found that some hens will go straight into the box and stay there, allowing the cock to feed them but not coming out so that the mating act can take place. I fully believe that this is the cause of a lot of infertile (clear) eggs, a warning to novice breeders that they should not be too anxious to get their birds nesting.

When I install the nesting boxes I always sprinkle some coarse soft pine sawdust on the concave bottoms. This is done for two reasons—first, it prevents the eggs from moving too freely in the hollow, running the risk of being cracked or dented. Second, sawdust helps to absorb any excess moisture from loose droppings which could foul the eggs and spoil them. Some hens will not tolerate anything in their box while the eggs are there, but when the chicks arrive they become far less fussy and are willing to accept the sawdust.

## Number of eggs

The sizes of the clutches will vary from three eggs to ten, the average being five or six. The eggs are laid on alternate days. This means that there may be a difference of some ten days between the hatching of the first and last egg of a clutch. Since the period of incubation is 17 to 18 days, it may take nearly a month from the laying of the first egg to the hatching of the last.

I have often been asked why the eggs of budgerigars could not be removed as they are laid, as is done with canary eggs, and then replaced when the clutch is complete. However, this does not seem to be practical. Nature has arranged for this difference in age so that the burden of feeding the babies with special food direct from the crop is spread over a period of time, to reduce the strain on the parents. Before the last chicks are hatched, the first ones are ready to be fed partly digested whole seed.

I know that it is a constant temptation for the novice to peek into the nest boxes, but he should do this only infrequently, and always during the early part of the day. Some hens object strongly to any interference with their nests and, at times, have been known to go to the extreme of actually throwing out their eggs. A quick look every four or five days should be enough to keep the breeder in touch with what is going on.

LOUISE VAN DER MEID
Hand feeding baby birds is a difficult and exacting task.

# X   Rearing the Chicks

Do not expect every egg to hatch. Some may be clear (in-fertile) or some chicks may die in the shell for one reason or another. The novice should not be disheartened if this happens because, as with all livestock breeding, there are bound to be failures along with the successes. Clear eggs occur when one parent is not really fit, or when the hen has gone straight into the nest box without mating with her partner. Loose perches, as discussed on page 105, are also a cause.

## Dead-in-Shell

The reason for dead-in-shell—fully formed chicks being unable to escape from the egg—is not completely under-stood, and there is still much to learn about this unfortunate happening. However, many of the cases of dead-in-shell are due to an excessive drying out of the eggs, which causes the

HARRY LACEY

A fine Buttercup Yellow parakeet was developed during the 1930s, but fell from popularity after the Lutinos arrived on the scene. Lately there have been signs of a revival of interest in the color.

chicks to stick to the inner membrane, and keeps them from turning in the shell to peck their way free. Water sprayed periodically on the bottom of the nest box and on the hen herself will often prevent this, especially during excessive dry spells. Some breeders add lugol's solution to the drinking water, one drop to every gallon. Others believe dead-in-shell to be a nutritional deficiency and supplement the diet with vitamin B-complex, particularly riboflavin.

## Four Babies

If you are breeding birds for exhibition or breeding, you will want them to be fine healthy specimens of their variety, so it is important that they be carefully nurtured in the nest. For one pair of parents the number of babies should be limited to four. You will not of course destroy any eggs until they have all hatched and you are able to select the four strongest nestlings. These four are left with the natural parents. The others are farmed out to other parents—those whose nests contain less than four babies of about the same age—or if none is available, the nestlings will have to be painlessly destroyed.

Breeders of exhibition birds often deliberately breed pairs of more ordinary specimens to act as foster parents. Their less valuable eggs are removed and destroyed and replaced by the excess eggs of the more desirable birds.

The nestlings should, of course, be closed ringed *before* they are transferred to the new nest.

## Newborn Chicks

Parakeets are born almost naked, and blind. In about a week the down appears and then the feathers start to come in. The wing and tail feathers arrive first, and at three weeks the quills of the other feathers will start to form. A newborn chick can live without eating for about twelve hours, getting nourishment from a yolk sac protruding from its abdomen.

The eyes open in about six days, and at two weeks the nestling can raise its head and move about. The babies are completely feathered at about five weeks, and it is then they first venture out of the nest box. After emerging, they are mainly fed by the cock for the first few days.

When the fledglings are about three months old, their first molt will commence, and the adult plumage start to grow in. The pinkish-lilac ceres will become blue or brown, according to sex, and the bars on the head will recede. Adults usually molt in the autumn, but with captive birds, kept under unnatural heat and artificial light, the molt can vary greatly and sometimes there is no one molt at all, but several partial ones.

## Weight

When a chick hatches, it weighs about two grams ($\frac{1}{15}$th of an ounce), and a month later, when it is ready to leave the nest, it will have approximated its adult weight which, on the average, is 45 grams—a little over $1\frac{1}{2}$ ounces.

## Feeding Nestlings

As the eggs hatch, the chicks are fed by their mother four or five times an hour, day and night. In the beginning they lie on their backs waiting to be fed, but soon they are able to sit up and raise their wide-open mouths.

The mother feeds the newborn first, and then the others according to age, the oldest chick being fed last. This gives the youngest first chance at the crop milk, while the older ones get seeds in their diet.

## Crop Milk

For the first few days, newborn budgies are fed on a thick secretion rich in protein, known as crop milk since it is regurgitated from the mother's crop, although it is not true milk. As the nestlings grow older, partially digested seeds are added to the milk, and as time goes on, the babies are fed less milk and more seeds. While she is sitting on the eggs the cock feeds the hen, but when the chicks hatch both parents participate in feeding them.

## Sprouted Seed

Many aviculturists like to feed their newly fledged birds, after they leave the nest, on sprouted seed. The seeds usually used for this are oats (still in the husk), canary and wheat. Soak them in water for about 12 hours. Take a good-sized ceramic saucer or a tray. Put some water in the bottom and

The quality of the mantle (the area over the shoulder) decides whether an Opaline is a good-colored example or not. This bird has too much undulation. For best results, he should be mated to a bird with an extremely clear mantle.

cover it with several thicknesses of blotting paper, burlap or flannel cloth. Spread the soaked seeds over the moist surface. Place the tray in a warm spot, and continue to keep the seed moist (not wet) by adding water as it evaporates. When the sprouts—actually the seed germs—have grown to a quarter of an inch, feed them to the birds in treat cups. Sprouts are a good source of Vitamin E.

## Regular Seed

When babies are no longer being fed by the parents it is a good idea to crack their seed with a rolling pin for the first few days, and place it in a shallow saucer on the floor of the cage or flight since they may not have sense enough to find the regular hopper.

## Cleanliness

Just how often you should disturb the nestlings is debatable. The consensus is no more than absolutely necessary, once a day at the most. However, the eggs, the babies and the nest itself must be kept clean.

Eggs that are fouled with droppings should be gently washed with a rag dipped in warm olive oil, with the emphasis on the word "gently" since the eggs are so fragile.

The soft food on which the nestlings are fed sometimes dries on the beak and cere like plaster. This should be removed, or the upper mandible will develop more slowly than the lower, resulting in a deformed beak (see page 208). Hardened food can also get inside the upper mandible, with the same result unless it is removed with a toothpick.

The claws sometimes become clogged too, with fecal matter and food. Here again, warm olive oil should be used to remove it. Never try to just pick it off, or a toe may come with it.

The vent too must be kept free of hardened droppings; warm oil and a cotton tip swab will do the job here.

As soon as the first clutch leaves the nest, the concave block should be cleaned thoroughly or replaced with a new one, and the removal of this block at the end of the second round will signal the end of the breeding season. As I have said before, it is not wise to let the hen lay a third round of eggs, unless one or both of the first two rounds has been a failure.

## Water for Breeders

During the breeding season (and when molting), the parent birds need more water than they normally drink. They feed their young on crop milk which, though cream-like in appearance, contains a high percentage of water. Some breeders prefer to substitute cow milk for the drinking water during this period. They make sure, of course, that it is always fresh. If the babies are to develop properly, there must be an ample supply of crop milk. Some breeders believe a lack of crop milk to be a major cause of French Molt.

## Foster Parents

If either one of the parents should die while the babies are still in the nest, do not seek a foster parent. Leave the remaining parent alone and it will rear the young by itself. In fact, when the last of the second clutch of eggs has hatched and the babies are about two weeks old, many breeders remove the hen to prevent any further laying, and allow the cock to raise the nestlings by himself.

If both parents die, or if there are more than four babies to raise (unless the extra birds are destroyed), foster parents will have to be found. Most budgerigars raising babies will accept the eggs and nestlings from another nest provided they are about the same age as their own. A foster mother will accept the eggs from any other pair and raise them as her own.

## Sexing the Fledglings

When I put my youngsters into flights, I always endeavor to separate them by sexes as I believe in keeping them segregated until breeding time. I know that it is difficult for the novice to tell young baby cocks from hens, but if the following points are checked on, a very high percentage of the chicks can be correctly sexed.

Young cocks of the Normal, Opaline, Gray and Dominant Pieds invariably have more boldly rounded bluish-tinted ceres, whereas the ceres of the young hens of these varieties are more flat and rimmed with white. With the cocks of the

Red-eyed, Cinnamon and Recessive Pieds, sexing is more difficult because of the strange coloring of the cocks. Their ceres are a purplish-flesh shade and do not always differ greatly from those of the young hens. The main guide here is the boldness of the cocks' ceres. Young cocks of all colors are usually more inquisitive and inclined to be more playful than the young hens.

Another method is to deliberately let a fledgling nip your finger; at this age, the hen's bite will be stronger than the cock's. As you become more familiar with budgerigars you will be able to distinguish sex by the head formation, even when they are babies.

It should be realized, of course, that different birds develop in different ways, but after a time the breeder becomes reasonably proficient in sexing them, and as soon as the birds complete their first molt there will be no further difficulty, because the cock's cere is always blue or flesh colored, and the hen's buff or brown.

**Scientific Sexing**

Of interest to the zoologist, with implications for the advanced budgerigar breeder, is this new method of sexing birds developed by S. J. Biondo. He has tested it on macaws and cockatoos; it is quite possible that after further experimentation, it may be useful for the smaller members of the psittacine family.

Begin by very lightly rubbing a flat toothpick over the inside of the bird's cheek. Next, smear the cells onto a glass slide previously coated with a layer of egg albumin. Pass the slide through graded solutions of alcohol (beginning with 95% ethyl alcohol and ether) to distilled water and stain with a basic dye such as hematoxylin or cresyl violet. Finally, view the slide with a microscope: After examining about 100 cells, the diagnosis is male if Barr bodies (sex chromatin) appear in significant number in the interphase nuclei.

**Bands or Rings**

Pedigreed parakeets are banded for identification purposes.

Such bands are sold by the various budgerigar societies; they can also be purchased from private dealers. You will find their advertisements in the cage-bird magazines. There are two types of bands: the closed band (or as it is known in Britain "ring") made of aluminum, and the open one, made of plastic or aluminum. The closed band is placed on the baby bird's tiny leg soon after birth, and stays there for the rest of its life. Once the leg has grown the band cannot be lost or removed; the only way to get it off is to cut it off. The band bears the breeder's code, a number for the bird, and the year of birth.

Open bands can be put on at any time and removed at will; they come in many different colors. They are usually used for temporary identification purposes. Because of their color they can be seen from a distance and the bird identified without being caught.

## How to Band

It is difficult to give an exact time for banding since the feet and legs of individual birds vary. With some specimens, bands can safely be put on about the sixth or seventh day; with others it may be nine or ten days before they can be banded. After the bands are on, check them the next few days to be certain that they are still in place and adjusted correctly on the leg. The bands are usually put on like this:

The chick is held in one hand with one of its feet between the thumb and forefinger. The band is then slipped over the two longest toes and then along over the foot and up the leg, pulling the other toes through the ring with a small pointed bit of wood. The toes are flexible. I use the pointed end of a spent matchstick for this purpose, as it is less likely to do any damage than would a splinter of wood. Although the baby budgie may make a lot of noise while the banding is being done, it is more indignation than hurt, and once he is put back into the nest box, he settles down right away.

## Stock Books

As each band is used, its number should be carefully entered

This Opaline Cobalt cock mated with a Cinnamon Yellow/Green hen produced these two young, exact replicas of the hen, and four clear eggs in their first nest.

in a notebook, so that an accurate record is kept. These stock books, as they are known, can be quite simple, although specially printed ones are on the market. The main entries are the ring numbers, along with the colors of the parent birds, together with whatever is known of their age, ring numbers and ancestry. Other information that should be entered are the dates of the laying of the eggs, their hatching and when the chicks leave the nest. The clear or addled eggs should also be noted, and so should any peculiarities of the parents or the chicks themselves. Obviously, if there is any evidence of French Molt or undershot beaks (see page 207) in the offspring, this too should be noted.

## Leaving the Nest

The exact age when young birds will fly from the nest boxes, while variable, is usually between five and six weeks. Healthy birds can fly quite well as soon as they leave the boxes, but are dependent on their parents for another week or ten days

The six eggs in their second nest hatched and every youngster was an exact replica of the Yellow/Green hen.

for food. During this period they will learn to crack and shell seed, and when the last chick in the nest has been flying for about a week, it is safe to remove all the young from the parents and put them in a cage by themselves.

The adult birds can then proceed with their second clutch of eggs. If the young are not removed as soon as possible, they may damage the new-laid eggs, or be injured by their busy parents. I always house each family of youngsters together in a cage for a week or two so they can settle down, and keep a careful watch on their behavior before putting them into a flight where they can develop to their fullest.

## First Molt

The colors of young budgerigars are always less bright and pure than they are when the birds are fully grown. Consequently, it is not a good thing for the exhibition breeder to dispose of any young birds before they have assumed their adult plumage. Here again the molting period varies with individual strains and colors, the usual time being 12 and 16 weeks.

During the molt, and particularly the first molt, the young birds must be watched closely, as this is a crucial period in their lives. When they are "half dressed" as it were, they are most susceptible to chills, and may become run down. The birds must be kept constantly under observation, and at the first sign of sickness they should be immediately removed from the aviary and cared for in a cage of their own (see Chapter XV).

I have already pointed out that budgerigars must have plenty of gravel or grit and minerals at all times, and this is particularly important during the molting period. In addition to the various mixed grits, cuttlebone and mineral blocks, the birds should have crushed dried egg shells, raw crushed chalk, clean river sand or sea sand and freshly dug clean soil. All these mineral-containing elements help to provide the fledglings with the minerals needed to form strong healthy feathers, good bone and a sound body. It may not be possible to offer every one of these items, but as many as possible should be procured. They should be supplemented further by various fresh green foods as discussed in Chapter V.

Except for those birds intended for exhibition, all young budgies should be given as much flying space as possible, always keeping the sexes apart until they are to be readied for breeding.

## Aging

There is no way of judging the age of an unbanded adult bird if no records have been kept of its birthday, and once a baby bird grows into a young adult, it is almost impossible to distinguish it from a much older bird. (A closed band, of course, gives the year of birth.) In old age, the upper mandible and nails sometimes get brittle and grow faster, and the bird gets fat as he gets older. A few birds develop scales on their legs as they grow older, but this is not generally true of budgerigars. No cock over six, and no hen more than four years old, should ever be used for breeding.

This picture dramatizes the length of a parakeet's wings when fully extended ,which makes it such a swift flier.

# XI   Liberty Budgerigars—Flying Free

Some years ago, the late Duke of Bedford, an avid aviculturist, carried out a series of successful experiments in letting budgerigars fly free on his estates in England. Since that time, many other budgerigar enthusiasts have followed the Duke's example, and the establishment of aviaries of "liberty" or "homing" budgerigars, as they are known in the fancy— birds that return home like pigeons—has become an important division of the hobby. However, to say they "home" in the manner of pigeons is not quite correct; a pigeon can be driven many miles away in a closed truck, and will unerringly find its way back to the loft. A budgerigar does not have this instinct, but it does learn to remain in the immediate vicinity of its aviary and find its way back at nightfall.

It is a wonderful sight to see flocks of brightly colored budgies soaring through the air, playing in the trees and on the lawns. Although I have not had the opportunity of owning a stud of homing budgerigars myself, I have often enjoyed watching other breeders' flights at liberty.

## It Takes Time

However, do not expect this thrilling sight right at the beginning; it may take some time for your untrained budgie to get up enough courage to venture forth. This is particularly

This attractive loft could be converted to a "liberty loft" merely by arranging popholes under the sheltering eaves. This should be done on the side away from the overhead wire, which constitutes a hazard to low-flying budgies.

HARRY LACEY

true of those which have been bred and reared in cages, but since these are usually the rares, you will not want to risk their liberty anyway.

Although it was once believed that there were special strains of homing budgerigars, experiments have shown that this is not so; any budgie can learn to "home" provided it is housed in an aviary designed for this purpose, located in the right spot. By this, I mean suburban and rural areas. In heavily populated areas, there are too many adverse factors to risk freeing the birds. Liberty flying should never be attempted from city rooftops.

Obviously, you would not want to attempt the experiment with rare birds, nor with any birds you are planning to use for controlled breeding. I would suggest that you start out with young birds bred in colony aviaries, or birds purchased with just this purpose in mind. They must be confined to their special outdoor flight until they have become fully acquainted with their surroundings. I, myself, am inclined to think the best time is after the birds have mated and the hens are starting to incubate their eggs, as this gives both cock and hen an incentive to return to the nest. It is necessary, of course, that the nest boxes be kept in the flight, in clear view of the birds when they are flying free.

## Precautions

It is a good idea to identify your liberty birds with colored plastic leg bands, even if they are already closed banded, so that you can identify them from a distance.

Food, water and all the other appurtenances should be protected under cover, but still left in full view of the birds. If seed is left unprotected, it can be blown about by wind and spoiled by rain. While at liberty, of course, the birds are able to forage for their own green foods and weed seeds, and this too is a point to be considered if there are farms or gardens in the neighborhood. However, unless your "liberty" flock is large, I doubt there will be any noticeable depreciations and the pleasure of seeing "wild budgerigars" in their gardens will more than compensate most neighbors.

Nevertheless, you should let them know in advance what

you are planning; otherwise they may attempt to capture your birds, thinking they are strays. A notice to this effect in your community news may also help. If any damage is done, be prepared to make amends. Also, keep on good terms with the children in the neighborhood. You never know when you may have to call on them to help find missing birds.

## It's a Cliffhanger

The first time you watch your birds taking off from the aviary, you will do so with a heavy heart. It will be thrilling to see them flying about, perching on trees and bushes, nibbling at bark, rolling in the grass, and exciting trying to keep tabs on them, but when you see them circling upward and going out of sight, the heavy lump may settle in your stomach.

It goes without saying that you are going to lose some birds, and not necessarily the first time out. As they become bolder, they will fly farther and farther away, and if they have no good reason for returning (food or the "parental" urge), they may not come back at all. Too, they may meet with an accident, or be captured by someone who assumes them to be strays. But some will return, and these will become the foundation of gradually increasing generations of "liberty" budgies.

There is also the pleasant possibility that some of those who don't return will learn to forage for themselves, will breed and multiply, and establish wild colonies of budgerigars in your community, so you will still be able to enjoy them— even if they never come home again.

It has been estimated that the great majority of these budgerigars allowed their freedom travel no more than 200 yards away from the aviary; the bold ones will go as far as a mile, but they, too, can find their way home if there are prominent landmarks.

## Color Varieties

Although budgies of any color can be kept at liberty, the

red-eyed albino and semi-albino birds are not likely prospects, since their eyesight is less keen. When domesticated birds fly free, all their senses should be working at their fullest. Nor do I think that the greens make good "liberty" birds because of their protective coloring; nor are olives, grays and mauves much better. Choose the brightly colored birds, those easily seen in flight and among the trees—Yellows, Cobalts and Opaline Blues, for instance.

## Pophole

The chief difference between a regular outdoor flight, as described in Chapter IV, and a liberty aviary is the pophole, or trap, through which the budgies leave and return. It should be a hole about six inches wide in the roof, or on one side just below the roof. It should be at the end of the flight furthest from the shelter.

Do not simply cut a hole in the wire and let it go at that. You will have to edge it with a wooden ring or hoop so that the jagged ends do not injure the birds.

Do not have more than one hole, as too many will make it more difficult to keep the birds under control. It is important to have the hole up high, or the birds will hesitate to use it. There must be a means of closing the trap when you

As he comes in to land, he extends his legs and retracts the wings slightly, to slow his air speed. The stained vent feathers indicate an upset stomach.

want to keep the birds inside. Possibly the best thing for this is a $\frac{1}{2}$-inch wire mesh cone, or funnel, about $3\frac{1}{2}$ inches long, stuck down into the hole. Its mouth should be $5\frac{3}{4}$ inches across—just enough to fit into the opening—tapering down to $1\frac{1}{2}$ inches at the bottom. The birds enter the wide mouth of the funnel and go head first out the narrow end, but find that end too small to use as an egress. Once all the birds are safe inside at night, you can slide a mesh or solid panel door across the opening. The funnel, of course, should not be put in place until late afternoon, as you will want the birds to feel free to go in and out at will.

In the morning, when the birds are ready for their day's outing, slide open the port and remove the mesh cone. (In the summer, this should be quite early in the morning, but in winter it should be early afternoon; and never at all when the weather is threatening.)

Replace the cone with a small ladder of tiny perches leading down from the hole to the top of a feeding platform about 14 inches square. This should be raised up to within 18 inches or so of the pophole; it can be supported on the top of a post rising from the floor of the flight, or on a shelf built in from one side of the flight and directly beneath the trap.

Keeping their favorite seed or spray millet on this raised platform will help to attract the birds back. It will also attract other birds, especially sparrows, and these can present a minor problem if they get inside the aviary. However, they usually take off in a hurry whenever a human being draws near.

There is not much you can do about the wild birds feeding from the budgies' seed tray. However, keep it in mind and add extra seed to make sure your birds get their share. The feeding tray can be of wood, but possibly the best material is plastic with tiny holes punched into it to allow rainwater to drain off. (Wetting seed does no harm.) Nor should this tray be the only seed vessel in the aviary; there should be at least one more inside the shelter.

Keep a stepladder, or if the roof is not too high a two-step, outside the aviary to enable you to open and close the trap, and to insert and remove the funnel and bird ladder.

Another way in which the liberty flight differs from the

regular flight is that there should be several landing platforms on the roof; birds at liberty will spend a great deal of time sitting on the roof of the aviary, or in nearby trees. It is wise to put an edging of board or plywood all around the edge of the flight—as a matter of fact, these boards can be so arranged that wire catguards can extend from their undersides. It is also a good idea to have small "landing strips" all around the trap.

A birdbath in the garden is a good idea, not only to serve the budgies, but to attract wild birds as well.

## Rain or Shine

Budgerigars can withstand pretty bad weather; however, it is unwise to release them during a cold rain (a summer shower will do no harm), a snowstorm or in fog. Snow on the ground need not hold you back, as they can stand seasonable cold—the main problem is to keep their feet from freezing.

## Cat Dangers

One of the major problems with keeping budgerigars at liberty is the cat. If you have one that prowls freely around the aviary, or if there are neighbors' cats roaming your premises, the chances of maintaining a liberty aviary are not too good.

The birds will have to be protected, not only when they are flying free, but also when they are inside the aviary, if a cat or rat (or for that matter a predatory bird) can get into the flight the way the birds get out. We have discussed cat and rat proofing in Chapter IV, but in the case of liberty aviaries, we have to go even further. Since many budgies will light on the top of the flight before they enter, cats must be kept off the roof. The best way to do this is with a width of wire around the entire top of the aviary and the shelter, extending out like the brim of a garden hat. The hole through which the birds go in and out should also be protected; netting with mesh large enough to let budgies through, but keep cats out, will have to be placed over the hole when the funnel is not in place.

Nor should there be a tree nearby from whose overhanging branches a cat can leap to the top of the aviary, or pounce on any birds perched there. This can create a problem, in that there should be a tree close to the aviary on whose branches the birds can light when entering and leaving. Perhaps a sapling or big bush, whose branches are strong enough to support a bird but not a cat, is the answer.

An ever-present peril is that if the birds see a cat close by, they will not return to the aviary, or if they are already inside, they will be afraid to go out.


**Flyaways**

Having pointed out to you the fun of keeping budgerigars at liberty, I feel duty bound to come up with a few suggestions for recapturing lost or strayed birds. Obviously, the closed bands or plastic rings you will have placed on the birds' legs will identify them as yours, and a record should be kept on file.

Once spotted, a reluctant budgie must be enticed into a "trap." Frequently, a live decoy will help accomplish this and if you can use the bird's mate, so much the better. Get as close to the bird as you can without frightening it, and set the cage with the decoy on the ground and a small empty cage, whose open door is on ground level, beside it.

Put some seed on the floor of the cage, and move some distance away. The stray bird will be attracted by the chattering of the decoy and will investigate; soon the chances are good that it will enter the cage to get seed. When he does, approach softly from the same side as the door and quickly close it. The bird is more likely to flutter upward in panic than to head instantly for the door. Of course, if you can rig up the door on a string so that it can be lowered from a distance, so much the better.

Another trick, if you do not have a decoy, is the old schoolboy trick of a wooden box raised at one end, with a peg to which a long length of fishline is attached. A millet spray is placed under the box, and when the stray enters to get it, the string is pulled and the dropping box traps the bird.

An Albino hen with her two Opaline offspring; one Sky Blue and one Cobalt. The other occupants of the nest were two Albinos. This indicates that the father is a split Albino.

# XII   Color Varieties

What color parakeet would you like to own? Perhaps you wonder about the correct name for your own particular pet. Word descriptions are inadequate, and an artist's conception is often not true to life. For your enjoyment and information, we have prepared what we believe to be the most comprehensive catalogue of color photographs of parakeets. Not all of these birds are show winners, but all of them are faithful representatives of their particular color variety.

In addition, we have prepared some notes covering distinctive features of various varieties.

## Normals

The Green, Yellow and Blue birds commonly offered for sale are called "Normals." Their feet may be either blue or pink; the eyes are dark with light irises; the cere of the male is blue while that of the female may be whitish blue, buff or brown; the beak is horn colored.

## Graywings

Graywings may have pink or blue feet; their eyes are dark with a light iris ring; the cere of the male is blue, that of the female whitish blue, buff or brown; the beak is horn colored.

## Fallows

These have an orange horn beak. There are two races or strains. One strain has solid bright red eyes, the other has red eyes with a light iris ring; the cere of the male is purplish-flesh colored, that of the female pallid flesh, buff or chocolate brown.

## Lutinos and Albinos

These are not true colors in themselves; these birds carry factors that suppress all other colors. This means that a Lutino is a yellow form of one of the Green series birds, and an Albino is an albino form of one of the Blue series birds, which includes the Yellow-face Blues.

The beak of the Lutino is bright orange horn, its eyes are red with a light iris ring, and the cere of the male is purplish-flesh colored, while that of the female is pallid flesh, buff or chocolate brown.

## Lacewings

The eyes are dark red with a light iris ring; the beak is orange horn; the feet and legs are always pink.

## Clearwings

The beak is horn colored; the eyes are dark with light iris rings; the head, neck, mantle and wings are clear and free from the usual undulated markings with suffusions; the male cere is blue, that of the female whitish blue, buff or brown.

## Opalines

The beak is horn colored; the eyes are dark with light iris rings.

The special features of the Opalines are intensity of color of body and wings, with lack of intensity of markings on neck and head. The mantle is clear and of the same bright shade as the body. The cere of the male is blue, that of the female whitish blue, buff or brown.

## Cinnamons

Cinnamons are distinctive even in the nest. For the first week after hatching, the skin covering the closed eye of the baby shows a pinkish-purple shade, as opposed to the black shade of the non-Cinnamons and the red of the Fallows, Albinos, Lutinos and Lacewings. When the birds mature, the altered color of the eyes can still be seen when viewed at an angle in a good natural light. The Cinnamon or "pink" color of the eye is apparent in every budgerigar which has the Cinnamon character in his genetic makeup.

The feet and legs are always flesh pink, the beak orange horn.

Cinnamon is not a true color, but a genetic character which suppresses black. For example, when Cinnamon Whites and Cinnamon Yellows are examined closely, it will be seen that no black whatsoever appears on any part of their plumage; any faint markings that show will be of a light cinnamon shade. The cheek patches are also pale pinkish-silver, as opposed to the bluish-violet shades of the non-Cinnamon forms.

## Violets

The beak is horn colored and the eyes are dark with light iris rings; the legs and feet are usually blue, although occasionally they may be pink.

The Violet character does not produce a color on its own, but is always combined with another color variety. It is only when certain combinations of character are bred, that the beautiful visual Violet shades result. The Violet Cobalts, or as they are more frequently called, the visual Violets, are the only birds in the series which have a color which appears to the eye as a true Violet. With the other colors, the Violet is only a tingeing or suffusion which alters their actual coloring.

## Slates

This color is sex-linked, and like the Violet and Gray characters it has the effect of altering all the Green and Blue series birds having it in their makeup.

The Slate Green series birds are very similar to the Violet Greens. They may be distinguished from the Violet Greens by the fact that the cheek flashes are deep in color and quite

A back view of the first Pied budgerigar to be reported in the United States. As this is a valuable bird, he is being held carefully to insure that no harm comes to him.

dull, and that the undulations are also much duller than those of the Violet Greens.

The Blue series Slate has a distinct coloring of the body shade; the cheek flashes are a deep dull violet, and the undulations are also dull.

**Grays**

Like the Slate and the Violet characters, this is a mutation which is not a color in itself, but affects the color of birds carrying the character. While the Slate is sex-linked, the Violet and Gray characters are dominant.

Birds in the Blue series, carrying the dominant gray mutation, are various depths of gray; in the Green series they are various depths of a dull mustard green known in the fancy as Gray Green.

The beak of birds carrying the Gray characteristic is horn, and the eyes are dark with light iris rings.

One way of distinguishing birds carrying the Gray factor is the fact that the two long central tail feathers are either

A front view of the same bird.

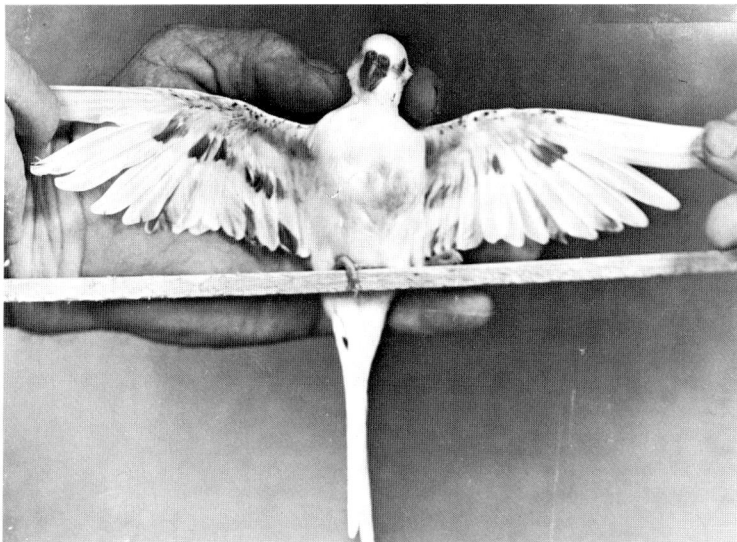

*jet black*, or *black* on the outer edges, light in the center, depending on the body color of the bird. These same tail feathers in other varieties are always blue.

The feet and legs are dark gray to pink.

## Pieds

These are divided into Recessive Pieds and Dominant Pieds according to their mode of color inheritance. The eyes of the Recessive (Danish) Pied are plum colored *without* light iris rings, while those of the Dominant Pied are dark with a light eye ring. This applies to all birds in the Green and Blue series. In the Green and Blue series of the Recessive (Danish) Pied, the beak is an orange horn color; the throat spots may range from a full complement to a single spot, or be entirely absent; the cheek patches may be normal to bright violet, silver or a mixture of both; the ceres of the cocks are a purplish-flesh like those of the Lutinos, while those of the hens are whitish-flesh, bluish-flesh to buff, and deep chocolate brown when in full condition.

There is a wide variation in the pattern markings, from birds showing only about 5% dark markings, graduating up to those showing about 80% dark markings. In general, the cock birds show the lighter markings, the hens the darker ones.

## Clearflights

When Clearflights are bred with the Recessive (Danish) Pied mutation, an entirely new type is produced. See page 163.

A Clearflight is dominant, but there can be great variation in the markings of these birds, ranging from perfectly patterned specimens to those showing just a small clear patch at the back of the head. In some specimens, the mask area tends to over-spill and extend part of the way down the upper chest and this is considered a fault for exhibition. There is a small patch (spot) at the back of the head. In the Green series, the flights and two of the central tail feathers are yellow; they are white in the Blue series. With many, the claws and lower toes are pink, with the rest of the toes and the legs blue, thereby continuing the variegated pattern of the plumage. In addition to the Greens and Blues, the Clearflight can also be had in all the other colors and varieties, with the exception, of course, of Albinos, Lutinos and other Pieds. The reason for this is easy to understand: such birds could not show the Clearflight pattern markings.

The beak is horn and the eyes dark, with the usual light iris rings.

## Dutch Pieds

Dutch Pieds are seldom seen. Their outstanding features are solid coloring on the wings and body, which distinguishes them from the broken Clearflight which invariably has grizzle markings on the wings, with some lessening of the depth of body color. Sometimes when Clearflights are bred, some of the chicks will show only slight light markings, while others will display an excess of light areas. The last are often erroneously called Dutch Pied. In actual fact, the genuine Dutch Pied is a distinct and quite rare mutation.

## Dominant Pied

The original Australian Dominant Pied was of the type known as Banded, because of a narrow clear band running across the breast from wing to wing.

In the Dominant Pied, the beak is horn and the eyes are dark with the usual light iris rings; the feet and legs are bluish-mottled, flesh colored or a mixture of both; the cere of the cock birds may be similar to the normal Light Green or a mixture of this and flesh pink. The ceres of the hens are the same as those of the Normal Light Greens.

Most specimens carry a head patch, but in exhibition birds this is optional. Generally, the two long central tail feathers are light, but normal dark feathers are not considered exhibition faults.

Some examples are marked exactly the same as Recessive (Danish) Pied forms, but they can always be distinguished by the color of their eyes, which have the dark pupils of the Normal with light iris rings.

Fallow White Cobalt

Fallow Light Green

Violet Cinnamon
Violet

Yellow-face Opaline Mauve
Opaline Cinnamon Sky Blue

The Australian Clearflight may be an offshoot of the original Australian Pied. This type is exactly the same as the Normal (or any other form), except that the flight feathers are clear. I believe the Banded Pied is most attractive because of its delightful pattern markings. The body should be a solid color, with a clear, well defined continuous band approximately $\frac{1}{2}$-inch wide around the middle, just above the thighs. Part of the wing edge to the butt, and all the flight feathers, should be clear.

## Dark-eyed Clear Yellows and Whites

These birds are absolutely pure white and pure yellow, with dark plum-colored eyes—not black! They are the second generation result of crossing the Dominant Clearflights and Recessive (Danish) Pieds. There is a slight variation in the depth of the clear yellow color, according to whether the birds are the Dark-eyed Clear form of the Light Green, Dark Green or Olive Green.

There are also Yellow-face Dark-eyed Clears, which show varying amounts of yellow color on their body; these are sometimes known as Dark-eyed Lemons.

The author looking over some Dominant and Recessive Pieds before arranging the final matings.

## Yellow-face Blues

Although these birds are called "Yellow-*face*," they also show yellow on wing butts and on the tail feathers. While they can be bred in both the Green and the Blue series, it is obvious they will be visible only on the blue kind. There can be a Yellow-face form of all the Blue series, no matter what the color shade may be.

The eyes are dark with light iris rings, and the beak is horn colored. The ceres of cocks and hens are the same as with the normal Greens and Blues. The Albino having a heavy Yellow-face overlay gives rise to a lemon-colored bird. With the Fallow Blues, strange green blues come into being. The Yellow-face character is also used to produce the brilliant composite form called Rainbow.

## Halfsiders

During breeding operations, still a differently colored bird may appear in the nest box. These are the Bicolors or Half-siders. With well marked Halfsiders, the line of demarkation is straight down the center, so that when the bird is viewed from one side it may look like a Cobalt, and from the other a Light Green. It may even be Red-eyed Lutino on one side, and Black-eyed Normal on the other. Not all Halfsiders have their colors evenly divided; some will only show patches of the second color in their plumage.

Halfsiders cannot be produced to order; they appear, from parents that have mixed color characters in their genetic makeup, due to a breakdown in the usual orderly cell division. Halfsiders bred together produce Normal birds, which when bred together still produce only Normals.

This is a complex subject and for a more detailed discussion of it I refer my readers to "The Cult of the Budgerigar" by W. Watmough.

## Longflights

Longflights are not considered desirable show specimens and as aviary birds they are not too acceptable, since their long

Graywing Olive Green

Opaline Gray Green

Opaline Dark Green
Cinnamon Light Green

Opaline Olive Green
Cinnamon Gray Green

Clearflight (Danish) Pied, Yellow and Green, Rainbow and Whitewing Blue.

The backs of the above birds.

flights and tails make flying difficult.

## Frizzled

Another mutation which occurred in Australia gave birth to birds with curled or frizzled feathers. Here again their flying is hampered by the feather formation, making them useless for aviaries. Like birds also appeared in England, but did not reproduce.

## Crest

This can be found in three different shapes—the Tufted, the Full Circular and the Half Circular. All of these can appear in all the different color varieties of budgerigars, and many attractive specimens can be and are bred. The Tufted carries a small erect crest of feathers up to about $\frac{1}{2}$-inch high, just above the cere.

The Full Circular Crest carries a neat round crest on the top of the head. This should drop evenly all around the head and cere.

The Half Circular Crest carries a half crest that drops over the front part of the head.

## For the Future

Although budgerigars have been produced in a very wide range of colors, breeders are still not satisfied and they are still striving, as they have for many years, to produce brown, red or black budgerigars. Whether or not they will be successful, only time will tell, but although many interesting experiments have already been carried out in all parts of the world, these three colors are still elusive. In my opinion, they will come into being only by a chance mutation, but since such mutations are always possible from any pair of birds, it may well be that the first of these mutations will occur in one of my readers' aviaries.

All six babies seen here are from a single nest. The possibility of getting numerous colors from a single breeding pair accounts for a great deal of the interest in the color breeding side of the budgerigar fancy. A knowledge of genetics is very useful.

# XIII   Color Inheritance

Breeding budgerigars for color is a fascinating hobby, and it gives the individual breeder a wide choice of colored varieties with which to experiment and breed composite types. After many years of breeding, I still find it exciting to put up a rather complicated pairing and get the results, or at least part of them, that I had anticipated. If the reader has not already indulged himself in a few unusual pairings, may I make the suggestion that one or two pairs be made up next season!

## Basic Genetics

To reproduce the colors discussed in the chapter on Color

Varieties may seem a very complicated matter, but it is not, once you grasp the basic principles of heredity. These statistical rules were first formulated by Gregor Mendel (1822–1884), an Austrian monk who carried out his experiments using garden peas. But it was not until 1900 when several biologists, working independently, confirmed them, that the implications of Mendel's discoveries dawned upon the plant and animal breeders of the world.

The color factors, and indeed all of the other factors that control inheritance in budgerigars, are transmitted by microscopic cell bodies known as chromosomes. These are in pairs of the same size, except for one pair—the sex chromosomes. On the chromosomes, like beads on a string, are minute bodies known as genes; these contain the different factors which will for the most part determine the physical appearance, and to a large extent the behavioral characteristics, of the offspring.

Genes are transmitted from the mother in the cytoplasm of the egg cell; also certain bacteria and viruses can be transmitted from mother to offspring, and while these are not genetic inheritances, they can influence the appearance and health of the young.

The female pair of sex chromosomes in birds is usually indicated by WZ (XY), and the male by WW (XX). As far as is known, the Z (Y) part of the female chromosome does not carry any special factor except that for sex.

The chromosomes split in two lengthwise, dividing the hereditary genes in half. Half of the mother's hereditary genes are in the ovum; half of the father's are in the sperm. The sperm meets and impregnates the ovum, and a baby is on its way. The new bird can inherit all kinds of characteristics from both parents, and the new bird's appearance is controlled by the group to which each factor belongs. In this chapter, we will discuss only the color characters and see how they operate.

## Mode of Inheritance

Color factors are inherited in either a recessive, an intermediate, a dominant or a sex-linked manner; as we shall

Olive Green Normal

Light Green Normal

Dark Green Normal
Yellowwing Light Green

Yellowwing Dark Green
Gray Green

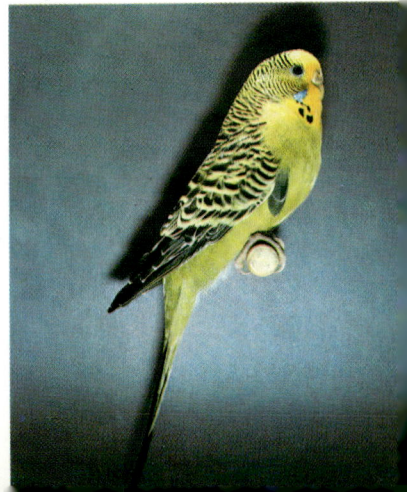

see, all these factors operate straightforwardly on Mendelian principles. For example, the original Light Green is, as would be expected, dominant to all other colors, but the actual tone of the green can be altered by certain other factors. Breeders now know that the following color factors are also dominant: Gray, Violet, Clearflight, Australian Pied and Dutch Pied.

A bird of one color can carry, hidden in its genetic makeup, the recessive factor for reproducing another color or colors. When it is mated to another bird carrying that factor, the color is brought out in the offspring. Such a bird, that is, one which is genetically hybrid, carrying within its genes characters other than those which it displays, is called *heterozygous*, or in budgie breeder terminology, it is known as a "split"— usually designated in writing by a diagonal line after the visible color: for instance, a Light Green that is "split" (that is, recessive) for Blue, would be listed as Light Green/Blue. The visible colors always appear first, followed by the hidden or recessive ones, for example, Sky Blue/Opaline Cinnamon White. The visible color is known as the phenotype. If a bird is carrying recessive characteristics which are masked by a dominant, these are part of the genotype. For example, the Light Green/Blue discussed above would be classified as Phenotype—Light Green; Genotype—Light Green split Blue.

All factors can be carried on either one or both halves of the birds' chromosome pairs, but a dominant character will make itself visible, even if it is on only half of the chromosome pairs. This is generally indicated, when writing down a dominant description (except Green), as being either a single factor or a double factor. The reason will be seen later. A single factor dominant is heterozygous, or split (to a recessive). A double factor dominant is genetically pure, or homozygous.

When, say, a Gray (single factor) is mated to a Sky Blue, half the young will be Gray (single factor), the other half Sky Blue, but if the Gray were a double factor, then all the young would be Gray (single factor), split to Blue, that is, carrying Blue as recessive. Another example is Australian Pied Light Green (single factor) mated to Light Green. Here half the young are Australian Pied (single factor) Light Greens, the other half Light Greens. The double factor

Australian Pied paired to a Light Green would give all single factor Australian Pied Light Greens. It must always be remembered that birds bred from a dominant and a recessive parent always show the dominant factor. It is never carried as a split.

The reason why some birds have a number of different color characters in their genetical makeup is that these various color characters can and are carried on different chromosome pairs. This makes it possible for birds to carry several characters in "split" form, or to be of visual composite color types.

**The Dark Factor**

The "intermediate" factor—only one is recognized at the moment—is called the "Dark" factor; it controls the shade or depth of the visible color. Neither the Light Green series nor the Sky Blue series, for example, possesses any of the Dark factor. When a single quantity of the Dark factor is added to these series, we get the Dark Green and the Cobalt forms respectively.

The Dark factor works differently from the dominant and recessive factors. A bird that possesses a single quantity of a dominant factor will display the dominant characteristic completely. The Dark factor, however, works by gradations.

When a double quantity is added, we get, respectively, the Olive Green and the Mauve forms.

The rules that govern this form of inheritance are worth bearing in mind, since they apply to all the different budgerigar mutations, where D equals the Dark factor and d the normal:

$$DD \times DD \text{ produces } 100\% \text{ DD.}$$
$$DD \times Dd \text{ produces } 50\% \text{ DD, } 50\% \text{ Dd.}$$
$$Dd \times dd \text{ produces } 50\% \text{ Dd, } 50\% \text{ dd.}$$
$$DD \times dd \text{ produces } 100\% \text{ Dd.}$$
$$Dd \times Dd \text{ produces } 25\% \text{ DD, } 50\% \text{ Dd, } 25\% \text{ dd.}$$
$$dd \times dd \text{ produces } 100\% \text{ dd.}$$

This Dark factor cannot be carried by birds of any kind in a split form; it always makes its presence visible through a difference in the depth of color. It will combine with any

Whitewing Sky Blue

Whitewing Cobalt

Cinnamon Sky Blue
Yellow-face Cobalt

Mauve Normal
Yellow-face Sky Blue Type II

other mutation; so that when any new mutation occurs, it can be had in three depths of shade in both the Green and the Blue series. Obviously then, the total number of color varieties has multiplied more rapidly than the actual number of mutations. Even now, in fact, though there have been very few new mutations in the last 25 years, there are still a considerable number of possible combinations that have not yet been bred.

## Breeding Splits (Recessives)

The recessive color factors often puzzle new breeders. As we saw, recessive color factors are those which, when paired with the wild type Light Greens, give only light green young. For example, if we mate a pure Sky Blue to a pure Light Green, we get all light green chicks, because Sky Blue is recessive to Light Green. The offspring, however, though green in appearance, differ from their Light Green parent in genetic makeup: they carry the possibility of producing Sky Blues if given suitable partners, and are known as Light Green/Blues (read as "Light Green split Blues"). If two of these Light Green/Blues are paired, their young will consist of 25% pure Light Green, 50% Light Green/Blue and 25% pure Sky Blue. The pure Light Greens and the Light Green/Blues will look just alike; to tell them apart you would have to breed them. (See chart at the end of this chapter.) The pure Light Greens and the pure Sky Blues will be as pure as if they had been bred from pure parents. These facts are useful to keep in mind when you are dealing with all the different kinds of cross-pairings of split birds.

Within themselves, the recessive color factors show degrees of dominance over each other, which, as I have said, can be puzzling. The normal Sky Blue (including Cobalt and Mauve) is dominant to all the other Blue series, and therefore can carry these other color factors in split form. While Sky Blue can be split for Graywing or White, it cannot be split for both at the same time—a bird must be either a Sky Blue/Graywing or a Sky Blue/White. Again, a Sky Blue can be split for Clearwing, but it cannot be split for Clearwing and White at the same time. These are points to remember when selecting breeding pairs.

## Breeding Graywing Splits

A Graywing can be split for White, but a White cannot be split for Graywing. Neither Graywing nor White can carry the Clearwing factor in split form, but a Clearwing can be split for White, and many of them are.

An unusual thing happens when a Clearwing is crossed with a Graywing: a new form is created, known as the Full Body Colored Graywing. These birds show visibly the color features of both parents, having the gray wings of the Graywing and the deep body color of the Clearwing. When mated back to Graywings, they breed Graywings and Full Body Colored Graywings; when mated to Clearwings, they give Clearwings and Full Body Colored Graywings. However, when mated to ordinary Whites, they give only Clearwings and Graywings—both split for White, of course. It follows then that all of the different recessives mentioned can be split for White.

## Breeding Recessives

To reproduce any of the recessive colors, both parents must have the factor in their genetic makeup. The following rules govern the mode of inheritance:

1. Recessive × Recessive = 100% Recessive
2. Recessive × Dominant = 100% Dominant/ Recessive
3. Dominant/Recessive × Recessive = 50% Recessive, 50% Dominant/Recessive
4. Dominant/Recessive × Dominant/Recessive = 25% Dominant, 50% Dominant/Recessive, 25% Recessive
5. Dominant/Recessive × Dominant = 50% Dominant, 50% Dominant/Recessive

There is at least one variation from these rules: When the Recessive (Danish) Pied is crossed with the dominant (single factor) Clearflight, the young are either Normal or Clearflight, both split for Recessive (Danish) Pied. If these Clear-

Recessive Pied Olive Green

Dominant Pied Opaline Green

Aus. Dominant Pied Opaline Gray Green
Dominant Pied Green

Australian Banded Pied Green
Australian Pied Opaline Olive Green

flight/(Danish) Pieds are mated back to (Danish) Pieds, they produce Normals, (Danish) Pieds, Clearflights and a new type—the Dark-eyed Clear. From this, it would seem that the Dark-eyed Clear is in actual fact a (Danish) Pied form of the Clearflight, since the birds have the eye color of the recessive Pieds. Now, when a Clearflight is mated to a Normal, the young are either Normal or Clearflight, again with both split for (Danish) Pied. These Dark-eyed Clears are very attractive birds, and can be had in White, Yellow and Yellowface White forms.

The fourth form of inheritance, called sex-linked, is one that you may find a little hard to understand until you have mastered the governing rules, which I am about to explain.

## Sex-Linkage

Many fanciers find real fascination in breeding the sex-linked varieties.

How well I remember the first sex-linked Lutino when it came to England, and the excitement and speculation it caused in budgerigar breeding circles. At that time we had no experience with sex-linked inheritance, and it took some time before its full implications were understood.

Sex-linked colors are, as the term suggests, colors linked to sex chromosomes, which accounts for their particular manner of inheritance. Sex-linked characteristics may be carried by one sex and manifest itself in the other; for example, hemophilia in humans, which is transmitted through the female but affects only the male. Because of the way budgies pass on their color factors, it is always far simpler to produce hens for a wanted color than cocks.

Chromosomes, as mentioned earlier, come in like pairs. The sex chromosomes, however, differ. In mammals, males have a pair of chromosomes designated XY, and females an XX. Therefore, sex is determined by the male. If he passes along the X chromosome, this pairs up with one of the female's X chromosomes and the new individual is a female. If he passes along a Y chromosome, this pairs with an X chromosome from the female and the offspring is a male.

In birds, though, the female determines the sex, because

she carries a WZ (XY) pair of sex chromosomes and the male has a pair of ZZ (XX).

Characters which are coupled, or linked, to the sex chromosome are called sex-linked characteristics. When they are on the W(Y) chromosome, only females will show this characteristic, because only they have one W(Y) chromosome.

When the characteristic is linked to the Z (X) chromosome, then for a male to show the characteristic it must be present on both of his ZZ (XX) chromosomes, that is, he must receive it from both parents. As mutant characteristics are usually recessive, if he only has it on one Z (X) chromosome, the other chromosome acts to suppress its appearance. The female would show the characteristic only if her single Z (X) gene is dominant to the W (Y) gene.

Now, let's see how this can work out in practice: If, for example, a Cinnamon cock is mated to an Opaline hen, all of the Cinnamon offspring will be hens, and all of the cocks appear Normal but actually be split Opaline and Cinnamon. If an Opaline cock is paired with a Cinnamon hen, all of the young hens will be Opalines, and all of the young cocks will appear Normal, but be split Opaline and Cinnamon.

## Sex-linked Color Expectation

The rules that follow apply equally to the six different sex-linked kinds, the Albinos, Lutinos, Opalines, Cinnamons, Slates and Red-eyed Lacewings. When two sex-linked kinds are paired together, the hen acts as though she were a Normal.

1. Sex-linked cock × Sex-linked hen = 100% Sex-linked cocks and hens.
2. Sex-linked cock × Non-linked hen = 50% Non-linked/Sex-linked cocks, 50% Sex-linked hens.
3. Non-linked cock × Sex-linked hen = 50% Non-linked/Sex-linked cocks, 50% Non-linked hens.
4. Non-linked/Sex-linked cock × Non-linked hen = 25% Non-linked/Sex-linked cocks, 50% Non-linked cocks and hens, 25% Sex-linked hens.
5. Non-linked/Sex-linked cock × Sex-linked hen = 25% Non-linked/Sex-linked cocks, 50% Sex-linked cocks and hens, 25% Non-linked hens.

## Working Genetics

Bearing in mind how the many color and pattern factors are inherited, I will try to show how they actually work. I have already given details of the simple Light Green to Sky Blue matings. I have also explained how the Dark factor is inherited in normal, straightforward pairings. There are, however, certain cases where, although the total number of green and blue-colored birds is the same, there is a different distribution of the Dark factor.

With some pairings, the Dark factor has a special linkage with the Blue, and consequently more Dark Blue (Cobalt) birds are bred. From other matings, the Dark factor is closer to the Green and more Dark Green birds result. These special linkages happen only when the Blue factor is involved, and it applies to Dark Green shades of all varieties.

This knowledge is useful to the breeder who wants to produce a preponderance of Cobalt stock. Those birds that give the larger number of Cobalts are called Dark Green/Blue Type II, and the others are known as Dark Green/Blue Type I. The percentages from these different matings have been worked out over a very large number of test pairs, and are as follows:

1. Dark Green/Blue Type II × Sky Blue gives $43\%$ Light Green/Blue, $7\%$ Dark Green/Blue, $43\%$ Cobalt, $7\%$ Sky Blue

The overall total is $50\%$ blue-colored and $50\%$ green-colored, with six Cobalts to one Sky Blue, and six Light Greens to one Dark Green.

2. Dark Green/Blue Type I × Sky Blue gives $43\%$ Dark Green/Blue Type I, $7\%$ Light Green/Blue, $43\%$ Sky Blue, $7\%$ Cobalt.

In this pairing, the shades of color are just the opposite from the first. This particular method of color inheritance also operates when the Cobalt and Mauve series are used, and is particularly valuable to specialist color breeders.

By the way, most breeders find that when green-colored birds are crossed with blue-colored birds, both kinds maintain the depth of their body shade. Another thing: with individual pairs, the percentages above will vary, but over a large number of matings they work out to be accurate.

When Cobalts are paired, they do not breed all cobalt-colored young, because their genetic makeup has an intermediate inheritance of the Dark factor. The only pairing that gives 100% cobalt-colored young is the pairing of a Sky Blue and a Mauve (see the rules on page 160). Cobalt to Cobalt gives 25% Sky Blue, 50% Cobalt and 25% Mauve. Mauve to Cobalt gives 50% of each, as does Sky Blue to Cobalt.

The Green kinds work like this: Dark Green to Dark Green gives 25% Light Green, 50% Dark Green and 25% Olive Green. Olive Green to Dark Green gives 50% of each, as does Light Green to Dark Green.

With these few rules, breeders can figure out what to expect from the majority of matings, since all varieties follow the same rules of inheritance.

## Yellows

We have seen how the Green, Blue and Dark factors work out; now we will include the Yellow in our calculations. As we have already seen, the Yellow factor is recessive to the Green, and when the two are paired, all the young are Green/Yellow. A Green/Yellow paired back to a Yellow will give 50% Yellow and 50% Green/Yellow. Two Green/Yellows paired together will give 25% pure Yellow, 50% Green/Yellow and 25% pure Green.

If a Yellow is paired to a Sky Blue, all the young will be Light Green, but they carry a special feature and will produce the double-recessive White, if correctly mated. That's how the very first ones came into being, in a mixed aviary of Greens, Blues and Yellows, and it was some time before the full implication of the cross was understood. When two of these Green/Whites (as they are now named) are paired, they breed no less than nine different types, including the White in the ratio of 1:16. A Green/White and a White give 25% Whites. If the Dark factor is introduced into the matings, then Whites with suffusions of Cobalt and Mauve are bred.

When the Dark factor is included in the Yellow kind, the Dark Yellows and Yellow Olive come into being. These

Lutino

Yellow Normal

Yellow-face Gray
Cinnamon Gray

Gray Normal
Dark-eyed Clear White

are very interesting birds: with care, you can use them to breed birds with a strong orange shade. In the first crosses, Dark Yellows can be of great use: by mating them to Olive Greens, you will breed Olive Green/Yellows. Mating two Olive Green/Yellows gives 25% of the desired Olive Yellows, from which you can choose pairings.

## Breeding Graywings

Graywings can be had in both the Green and the Blues series and, as explained on page 160, in two depths of every color: Dark and Normal Graywings.

Graywing Light Greens are recessive to Normal Light Greens, but dominant to Light Yellows, so a Graywing Light Green paired to a Light Green will give all Light Green/ Graywings, while a Graywing Light Green paired to a Light Yellow will give all Graywing Light Green/Yellows.

Graywings are not, as might be thought, an intermediate stage obtained by pairing Light Green to Yellow; they are the result of a definite mutation. It is not possible to breed Graywing Yellows—that is, birds with gray wings and yellow bodies—from any of the above pairings, but Graywing Yellows have been bred in Australia and the strain has been fixed. Odd specimens have turned up in British birdrooms. So far, I have seen only the feathers of the Australian Graywing Yellows, but they seem to be a clear-cut mutation, and one that might well have been expected.

If the Blue factor is introduced to Graywing Greens, Graywing Blues can be produced. There are two ways to do that. One way is to pair a Graywing Light Green cock or hen to a Sky Blue, which gives all Light Green/Graywing Blues. These can be paired among themselves or to Whites. If paired among themselves, they produce a small number of pure Graywing Blues; paired to Whites, they produce a larger number of Graywing Blue/Whites. The other way is to pair Graywing Greens to Whites, thereby getting all Graywing Green/Whites. These can then be mated back to Whites, giving Graywing Green/White, Graywing Blue/ White, Yellow/White and White.

A great many of the present-day Graywings are split for

White (or Yellow); when they are paired to Normals, only half their young carry the Graywing factor; the other half carry White (or Yellow). Therefore, when these split Normals are paired to Whites again, only half of them can produce actual Graywings.

This fact used to give rise to misunderstandings when the breeder thought all the young, other than the Normals, were Graywings. I have seen many Whites and Yellows disposed of as Graywings in all good faith, because the breeder knew they had a Graywing grandparent. If you study this chapter carefully, you can keep from making such mistakes.

So far, I have dealt with simple dominant and recessive pairings, where all the birds have normal-colored eyes. Now I will discuss the recessive type with red eyes, known to budgie fanciers as the Fallow.

## Breeding Fallows

The red-eyed variety called Fallows are pallid-colored recessives. All the other recessives, including Whites, can be split for Fallow. The only other recessive variation that can be carried in split form by White is the Recessive (Danish) Pied factor.

The very first red-eyed Fallow mutation occurred in America, but unfortunately the strain was not established. A year or so later, a similar mutation appeared in Germany; this time it was established and was soon being bred in both the Green and the Blue series. After the German Fallows had been in existence for some years, another type appeared in Great Britain. These birds were named English Fallows to distinguish them from the German.

Both types are very similar in general coloring, but their eyes are different. The German Fallows have deep red pupils with light iris rings; the English have solid red eyes without the light rings. Over the years, several other Fallow mutations have appeared in different parts of the world, but their relationship to the two established forms has not yet been fully explored.

When these two red-eyed varieties are paired together, the breeder gets quite a shock: all the young are normal in

Graywing Sky Blue

Graywing Mauve

Graywing Cobalt
Opaline Sky Blue

Yellow-face Graywing Sky Blue
Opaline Cobalt

color with black eyes. These normal-looking birds are split for both kinds of Fallow and will breed German Fallows when mated to German Fallows and English when mated to English. This shows quite clearly that these two Fallow mutations are recessive, quite separate, and independent of each other.

The rules that control their manner of inheritance are as follows and can be used for both English and German:

1. Fallow × Fallow = 100% Fallow.
2. Fallow × Normal = 100% Normal/Fallow.
3. Normal/Fallow × Normal/Fallow = 25% pure Normal, 50% Normal/Fallow, 25% pure Fallow.
4. Fallow × Normal/Fallow = 50% Fallow, 50% Normal/Fallow.
5. Normal × Normal/Fallow = 50% Normal, 50% Normal/Fallow.

There can be a Fallow form of all the other colors and varieties, and some very interesting and strange-colored birds can be bred with careful mating. If the Light Yellow form of the Fallows is bred and then the Cinnamon factor is added, the resulting young are similar to Lutinos, having red eyes and an almost clear yellow color. A kind of White can be bred using the Fallow-White-Cinnamon combination, and they look like Albinos. These elaborate combinations are useful and interesting, though the birds they resemble, Lutinos and Albinos, are far easier to breed.

Much more beautiful birds can be produced by selection of the Fallow Olive Green and Fallow Olive Yellow kinds. I have bred many examples of both in the German and English forms and find that the German Fallows have a far richer and brighter color. The Fallow Olive Greens show an almost pure orange-yellow shade on the breast and underparts, with a more orange-olive green tone on the rump set off by cinnamon-brown undulations. The Fallow Yellow Olives are, I think, even more attractive in their coloring: they have an overall rich orange-yellow color with only very faint cinnamon undulations, and the whole color seems to glow.

If the dominant Gray and the sex-linked Opaline factors are added to the recessive Fallow, a further unusual composite bird is evolved: the Opaline Fallow Gray. There the Gray factor has the effect of further lessening the already weak Fallow body color, but increasing the strength of the undulation. When the Opaline factor is added, the body color becomes a white gray, and the undulation on head, neck and mantle almost disappears, leaving the wing markings standing out strongly. Not many examples of this particular combination have been produced, but specimens do appear in experimental aviaries from time to time.

When the Violet factor is introduced into the Fallow Blue series, it is possible to breed some strange pallid body colors, particularly so with the Cobalt and Mauve kinds. The two examples of the Fallow Violet Mauve that I bred had slightly darker undulations than the normal Fallow Mauve, with the upper chest a pale red-brown mauve that deepened at thighs and rump.

The history of these two Fallow Violet Mauves is quite interesting, and it shows how colors can turn up when least expected. From the mating of a Fallow Cobalt cock to an Olive Green/Fallow Blue I bred, among others, a nice Olive Green hen. At that time I had a number of breeding pairs of split Fallows and, as would be expected, I had a whole range of colors among their young, including a good-colored visual Violet cock.

When I had made up my pairs, I found that I had overlooked a mate for the Olive Green/Fallow Blue hen. Looking over my spare cocks, I saw that the visual Violet of uncertain pedigree was in first-class breeding condition. It seemed to me that the best thing to do was pair these two birds, and perhaps get a few rich-colored Violets. The birds were put into a breeding pen and took to each other right away. Very soon the hen was sitting on a clutch of five eggs; in due time all of them hatched. One was a visual Violet, two were Olive Green, one was Mauve and one was Dark Green—a Violet carrier, I think, judging by its color. The second nest gave four chicks: another Olive Green, a Cobalt and two Fallow Violet Mauves, both hens. This is another good instance of how individual nests can vary; it shows how recessive factors can be handed down unseen and unknown.

I think there are two reasons why the Fallows are not

popular with breeders. First, the birds are inclined to be small and, since they are recessives, they take several seasons to produce from scratch. Second, while the English Fallows have more substance than the German kind, they do not have the same richness of color; but I feel strongly that the Fallow varieties deserve a lot more attention than breeders have been giving them up to now.

## Violet Factor

The Violet factor in itself is not a separate color; it is expressed only in its visual violet shade when combined with Blue and the Dark factors. There can be a Green form, as well as the Blue form, in all the variations that have the Violet factor in their makeup. This factor is a dominant one, and its presence in single strength is visible in the plumage of the birds. However, some breeders have found that birds with a double Violet factor are somewhat richer in tone than those with only a single Violet factor.

The Violet factor, being dominant, will always be visible when carried, which puzzles some breeders when the Green kinds are being produced. I know it sounds strange to say a bird is a Violet Green, but it really means that the bird has the Violet factor in its makeup. In a similar way, we say a bird is a Graywing Green or a Fallow Green, using the word Violet, Graywing or Fallow as a prefix.

I have explained that the beautiful visual violet shade can only be seen when combined with a Cobalt form, so every visual Violet in every different variety must be a Cobalt kind. If you remember that, the inheritance of the Violet factor becomes simple and straightforward; it is governed by the same rules that govern the Dark factor, as explained on page 160.

Now I think it would be appropriate to give a few matings to show just how the factor is transmitted. If a visual Violet (single factor) is mated to a normal Sky Blue, the pairing will, theoretically, produce 25% Violet Cobalt (single factor)—these are the visual Violets; 25% Violet Sky Blue—these are birds with an altered blue color; 25% normal Cobalts, and 25% normal Sky Blues. These last two are of no more value for breeding Violets than Blues and Cobalts that have no Violet ancestry. This applies to all the various crosses where normal colors result.

If two Violet Cobalts are paired, the theoretical expectations are Blue, Cobalt, Mauve, Violet Blue, Violet Cobalt and Violet Mauve. Some of the Violet-carrying birds will be double factor Violets, but these will be produced only in small numbers. It will, I hope, be fairly clear that it is impossible to breed all Violet Cobalts (visual Violets) from mating together two Violet Cobalt parents. Readers may wonder if any mating will produce all visual Violets. Strangely enough, they can be produced from the pairing of a double factor Violet Mauve to a Sky Blue or the pairing of a double factor Violet Sky Blue to a Mauve. Both of these pairings give young that are 100% Violet Cobalt, single factor. Since the double factor birds are extremely rare, most matings will give only 50% visual Violets and 50% normal Cobalts. The reason why so few double factor Violets have been produced so far is that, generally speaking, all the Violet birds are on the small side, and breeders in their endeavors to improve their stock naturally mate them to good, robust, outstanding normal birds.

When a visual Violet is paired to, say, a Light Green, only green-colored young are produced, but these, or at least some of them, are different from the ordinary run of Green/Blues. Therefore the young from the mating of a single factor Violet Cobalt to a Light Green will be Light Green/Blue, Dark Green/Blue, Violet Light Green/Blue and Violet Dark Green/Blue. The actual colors of these last two differ from the ordinary forms of Light and Dark Green. The latter two types are both very unusual and attractive. When a Violet Light Green/Blue is mated to a Cobalt, the youngsters will be Light Green/Blue, Sky Blue, Dark Green/Blue, Cobalt, Violet Light Green/Blue, Violet Sky Blue, Violet Dark Green/Blue and Violet Cobalt. This mating gives a small percentage of the desired Violet Cobalt birds, but when Green is used in their production, the general coloring is of a more even and richer shade.

I think breeders will also realize that the Violet factor can easily be introduced into a strain by a Violet Light Green/

Halfsider: Recessive Pied Cobalt

Halfsider: Opaline Dark Green/Cobalt

Tufted Crest Sky Blue
Full Circular Crest Cobalt (with mane)

Full Circular Crest Cobalt
Tufted Crest Dark Green

Blue, for instance, without the owner's actually knowing that there was a Violet bird in the stud. Many times I have been called to examine Violet birds that appeared "miraculously" from ordinary colored stock, and every time I have been able to account for them by the fact that Violet Greens had been used for their breeding.

Once the breeder has introduced the Violet factor into his stock, many forms of Violet factor birds can be produced in both the Blue and the Green series. It is difficult to say just which of the visual Violets is the handsomest; much depends on the breeder's preference. I myself am attached to the Cinnamon Violet Cobalts with their lovely soft cinnamon-brown undulating markings and their warm, rosy-tinted violet body colors. In their production, the sex-linked Cinnamon factor is used; and since the Violet is dominant, it does not present much of a breeding problem. In actual fact it is possible to breed such birds for the first cross by, say, mating a Cinnamon Sky Blue cock to a normal Violet Cobalt hen; a percentage of Cinnamon Violet Cobalt hens will result.

The rules that govern the inheritance of the dominant Violet factor can be used in all kinds of matings that contain the necessary color factors.

1. Violet (s.f.)★ Sky Blue × Mauve gives 50% Violet (s.f.) Cobalt, 50% Cobalt.
2. Violet (d.f.) Sky Blue × Mauve gives 100% Violet (s.f.) Cobalt.
3. Violet (s.f.) Sky Blue × Cobalt gives 25% Violet (s.f.) Cobalt, 25% Violet (s.f.) Sky Blue, 25% Cobalt, 25% Sky Blue.
4. Violet (d.f.) Sky Blue × Cobalt gives 50% Violet (s.f.) Cobalt, 50% Violet (s.f.) Sky Blue.
5. Violet (s.f.) Sky Blue × Sky Blue gives 50% Violet (s.f.) Sky Blue, 50% Sky Blue.
6. Violet (d.f.) Sky Blue × Sky Blue gives 100% Violet (s.f.) Sky Blue.

★ s.f. = single factor
d.f. = double factor

7. Violet (s.f.) Cobalt × Sky Blue gives 25% Violet (s.f.) Cobalt, 25% Violet (s.f.) Sky Blue, 25% Cobalt, 25% Sky Blue.
8. Violet (d.f.) Cobalt × Sky Blue gives 50% Violet (s.f.) Cobalt, 50% Violet (s.f.) Sky Blue.
9. Violet (s.f.) Cobalt × Cobalt gives $12\frac{1}{2}$% Violet (s.f.) Sky Blue, 25% Violet (s.f.) Cobalt, $12\frac{1}{2}$% Violet (s.f.) Mauve, $12\frac{1}{2}$% Sky Blue, 25% Cobalt, $12\frac{1}{2}$% Mauve.
10. Violet (d.f.) Cobalt × Cobalt gives 25% Violet (s.f.) Sky Blue, 50% Violet (s.f.) Cobalt, 25% Violet (s.f.) Mauve.
11. Violet (s.f.) Mauve × Sky Blue gives 50% Violet (s.f.) Cobalt, 50% Cobalt.
12. Violet (d.f.) Mauve × Sky Blue gives 100% Violet (s.f.) Cobalt.
13. Violet (s.f.) Mauve × Cobalt gives 25% Violet (s.f.) Cobalt, 25% Violet (s.f.) Mauve, 25% Mauve, 25% Cobalt.
14. Violet (d.f.) Mauve × Cobalt gives 50% Violet (s.f.) Cobalt, 50% Violet (s.f.) Mauve.
15. Violet (s.f.) Mauve × Mauve gives 50% Violet (s.f.) Mauve, 50% Mauve.
16. Violet (d.f.) Mauve × Mauve gives 100% Violet (s.f.) Mauve.

**Rainbows**

The budgerigar that has caused the biggest stir in recent times is the Yellow-face Opaline Clearwing or, as it is more popularly called, the Rainbow; these birds have a lovely blend of bright colors in their plumage. With this type it is necessary to get the Yellow-face factor, which is dominant to the Blue series, combined with the sex-linked Opaline and the recessive Clearwing—in this case, the Whitewings. The actual pairings that give varying percentages of the desired Rainbows are many and varied, but certain pairings promise quicker results than others.

These days it is fairly easy to get Yellow-face types in most varieties, including the Clearwings and Whites; Opalines

Dominant Pied Sky Blue

Recessive Pied Mauve

Recessive Pied Yellow-face Mauve
Recessive Pied Cobalt

Australian Pied Cobalt
Aus. Banded Pied Yellow-face Cobalt

can be had in Clearwings, Whites, and Normal/Clearwings or Normal/Whites. With these last two you must be sure of the actual breeding of the stock you use; otherwise a season's breeding may be lost. If an Opaline Whitewing or an Opaline White cock is mated to a Yellow-face Whitewing, Yellow-face Opaline Whitewings (Rainbows) will result in the first crossing. Such a pairing will also breed split birds carrying the necessary Opaline factor, which can be crossed to the Rainbow hens the following season; both Rainbow cocks and hens will result. As can be imagined, the most popular and brilliant coloring is carried by the Yellow-face Opaline Whitewing Cobalts (and Violet Cobalts). The Rainbows are not great favorites with exhibitors, since they are usually on the small side; nevertheless, they are held in great esteem by those budgerigar enthusiasts who like to see brightly colored birds in their aviaries or to keep them as household pets.

## Yellow-face

The Yellow-face factor can be had in several different mutations, each varying in the amount of yellow coloring on the Blue birds. As they all inherit in a similar manner, I will discuss them as Yellow-face. When a Yellow-face Blue (single factor) is paired to an ordinary Sky Blue, half the young are Yellow-face Blues and half Sky Blues—quite a simple inheritance.

With one of the Yellow-face varieties, a rather unusual thing happens which mystified breeders for quite a time. The pairing of two single factor Yellow-face birds of this particular kind gives normal pure Sky Blues, single factor Yellow-face Blues and a small percentage of double factor Yellow-face Blues. Now the strange thing about the double factor birds is that they do *not* have any trace of yellow in their plumage; they look exactly like a normal Sky Blue. However, when such birds are paired to Sky Blues, *all* their young are Yellow-face Blues, single factor of course. Interesting experiments can be carried out with the Yellow-face kinds, since it is possible to breed a Yellow-face form of all the Blue kinds.

When the Yellow-face factor is combined with Green, it is understandably not visible; nevertheless, Green birds can have the Yellow-face character in their genetical makeup, and many excellent examples of the Yellow-face Blue series are bred through Greens. I believe that in certain cases where one of the Yellow-face mutations is used, it is possible to see a slight deepening of the yellow colors in the tail feathers of young birds in the nest.

## Red-eyed Lacewing

I have already explained the working of the sex-linked factors, but I have not made any specific mention of the red-eyed Lacewing kind. This was the last recorded mutation to occur in Great Britain. These birds have either white or yellow-colored bodies, and the characteristic light cinnamon markings and chocolate-colored tails. They follow the usual method of inheritance, making it simple to produce Lacewing hens. There can be a Lacewing variety of all the other varieties, but only Lacewing forms of the Normals show the coloring to its best advantage. Practically all of the Lacewing Blues—or Lacewing Whites as they are more commonly called because of their body shade—do not differ in this shade. With the Lacewing Greens or Yellows, there is a difference in the yellow tone, and the Lacewing Olive Greens show a much richer and deeper yellow throughout than the Lacewing Light Greens, with the Lacewing Dark Greens coming in between the two tones. I mention this because I feel that more emphasis should be given to the breeding of the richer and darker shades.

## Slates

Another sex-linked variety—quite an old one, although not seen much these days—is the Slate. Here again, Slates can be had in all the different Blue and Green series. Like the Violet, they cause an alteration in the actual visual shade. The Slate Blues have a definite dull slate-blue color, and are quite distinct from any of the other Blue shades. The Cobalt and Mauve forms are correspondingly darker, but all have the

Pied Cinnamon Sky Blue

Banded Pied Cinnamon Sky Blue

Aus. Banded Pied Opaline Sky Blue
Australian Pied Opaline Blue Type II

Recessive Pied Sky Blue
Recessive Pied Yellow-face Blue Type II

A full circular crest showing a good fall of feathers from the center of the head.

same characteristic slate shading. Their cheek flashes also are different, and their tails are definitely dark blue, and not black like the Grays. It is rather difficult for the newcomer to recognize the Slate Green series, but it can be done with a little practice, since their color tone is quite different from that of the ordinary Green birds.

## Crests

The various Crested factors are dominant, but their mode of inheritance is a little more complicated, since a number of modifying agents have to be dealt with to create the different shapes of crests. Generally speaking, it is more satisfactory to breed Crests by mating a Crest to a non-crested bird that had a Crest parent. Such birds are commonly known as Crestbred, and they certainly do seem to increase the number of actual Crests produced when they are mated to Crested birds.

Experimental work is now being carried out in Great Britain by the Crested Budgerigar Club, and these eager fanciers are doing a fine job of mapping the Crest inheritance, and at the same time they are expanding the popularity of the Crested birds.

## Keeping Records

In my opinion, it is important to keep accurate records of all breeding results every year, and whenever possible to band all the young birds with closed, year-dated rings. If that isn't possible, the young must be banded with split metal rings before they leave the nest, and their numbers recorded. It is only by keeping accurate records that you can make scientific matings, so as to know what to expect from any given pairing. Closed banding of budgerigars does help considerably in preventing too close inbreeding, and the unpleasant results that can come from it. The use of colored celluloid or plastic rings as a second method of identification is useful.

## Detecting Recessives

In the foregoing paragraphs I have tried to explain briefly and simply how the various color factors of budgerigars are inherited. With careful study you should be able to calculate the expectations from the various color crosses. Always bear

A good tufted crest.

HARRY LACEY

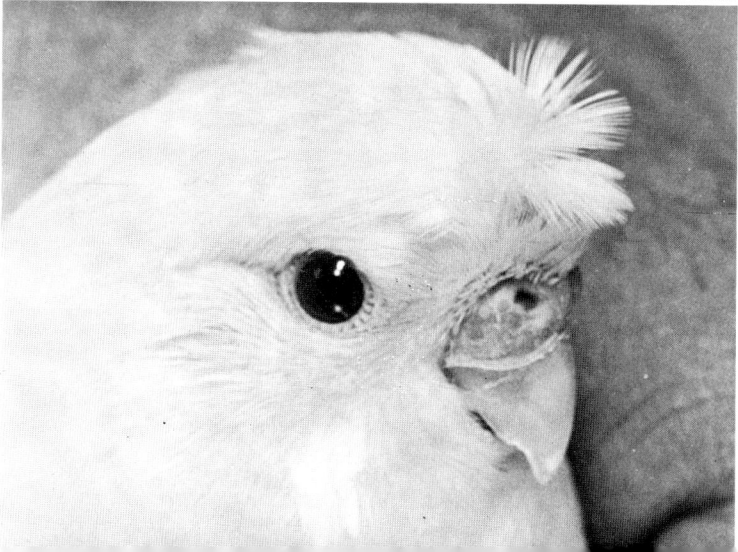

Dominant Pied Light Green

Dominant Banded Pied Opaline Lt. Gr

Pied Opaline Light Green
Banded Pied Light Green

Recessive Pied Light Green
Australian Pied Dark Green

in mind that when expectations are given, it is assumed that the birds are pure and not split for any other factor. When the expectations do not work out according to plan, it invariably means that unknown recessive factors have upset the calculations.

When odd colors appear from an apparently straightforward cross, the genetic makeup of the parents can be calculated by the color of the offspring. For example, if the breeder mates a normal-looking pair of, say, Sky Blues, and an Albino appears among their young, then it is certain that the cock is a Sky Blue/Albino and that the red-eyed chick will be a hen. Again, if a pair of Cobalts gives birth to Graywing youngsters, it is certain that at least one of the parents has the Graywing factor and the other either Graywing or White.

## Interpretative Breeding Chart

This simple chart, covering the Blue, Green, Yellow, Graywing, Opaline, Cinnamon, Lutino, Albino and White series birds enables you to determine the hidden recessives borne by the parents, based on the color of their offspring.

| Mating | Results | Explanation |
|---|---|---|
| (1)  Green × Green | Green | Normal results. |
| (2)  Green × Green | Blue | Both parents split Blue; one split Blue and one split White; or both split White. |
| (3)  Green × Green | Yellow | Both parents split Yellow; one split Yellow and one split White; or both split White. |
| (4)  Green × Green | White | Both parents split White. |
| (5)  Green × Blue | Green | Normal results. |
| (6)  Green × Blue | Blue | Green parents split Blue, or White. |
| (7)  Green × Blue | Yellow | Green parent split Yellow or White, and Blue parent split White. |
| (8)  Green × Blue | White | Both parents split White. |
| (9)  Green × Yellow | Green | Normal results. |
| (10) Green × Yellow | Blue | Green parent split Blue, or White, and Yellow parent split White. |

| Mating | Results | Explanation |
|---|---|---|
| (11) Green × Yellow | Yellow | Green parent split Yellow, or White. |
| (12) Green × Yellow | White | Both parents split White. |
| (13) Green × White | Green | Normal results. |
| (14) Green × White | Blue | Green parent split Blue, or White. |
| (15) Green × White | Yellow | Green parent split Yellow, or White. |
| (16) Green × White | White | Green parent split White. |
| (17) Blue × Blue | Blue | Normal results. |
| (18) Blue × Blue | White | Both parents split White. |
| (19) Blue × Yellow | Green | Normal results. |
| (20) Blue × Yellow | Blue | Yellow parent split White. |
| (21) Blue × Yellow | Yellow | Blue parent split White. |
| (22) Blue × Yellow | White | Both parents split White. |
| (23) Blue × White | Blue | Normal results. |
| (24) Blue × White | White | Blue parent split White. |
| (25) Yellow × Yellow | Yellow | Normal results. |
| (26) Yellow × Yellow | White | Both parents split White. |
| (27) Green × Graywing Green | Graywing Green | Green parent split for Graywing, White or Yellow. |
| (28) Green × Graywing | Blue | Both parents split for Blue. |
| (29) Green × Graywing Green | White | Both parents split for White. |
| (30) Green × White | Graywing | Green split for Yellow or White. |
| (31) Green × Green | Opaline Green | Cock split for Opaline. |
| (32) Green × Green | Opaline Blue | Cock split for Opaline and both split for Blue. |
| (33) Green × Green | Cinnamon | Cock split for Cinnamon. |
| (34) Green × Green | Cinnamon Blue | Cock split for Cinnamon and both split for Blue. |
| (35) Green × Blue | Cinnamon Blue | Cock split for Cinnamon Blue. |
| (36) Green × Green | Lutino | Cock split for Lutino. |
| (37) Green × Green | Albino | Cock split for Albino and hen split for Blue. |
| (38) Green × Blue | Albino & Lutino | Cock split for Albino. |
| (39) Blue × Blue | White | Both split for White. |
| (40) Blue × Blue | Graywing Blue | One parent split for Graywing and the other split for White or Graywing. |
| (41) Blue × Blue | Albino | Cock split for Albino. |
| (42) Yellow × White | Yellow | Normal results. |
| (43) Yellow × White | White | Yellow parent split White. |

188

This shows that the flight and long tail feathers of the French Molt birds are missing. They make good pets, but should not be used for breeding.

# XIV  Anatomy and Physiology

Perhaps it will be of interest to my readers to learn something of their budgies' anatomical structure and its physiology. This chapter is not intended as a text on anatomy, and no attempt has been made to treat this subject other than cursorily, with the thought that it might enable some of my readers to utilize this knowledge for their pets' proper maintenance.

## Skeletal Structure

Parakeets are birds of swift flight; consequently they have

tapering wings, long tails and strong muscles. The bone structure, like that of all birds, is light, strong and resilient. If the bones are examined carefully, it will be seen that while they are apparently fragile, they are strongly constructed and invariably rounded in shape. This is nature's way of giving strength while reducing weight. After all, the less he must lift, the easier it is for a bird to fly. Bones are built of various mineral elements, principally calcium, and it is essential that these elements be included in the birds' diet.

A bird's wing is like a modified human arm. I realize that you cannot examine the bones of a parakeet's wing too closely, but the bones of a chicken wing are much the same and readily available. You will find that the "upper arm" is a large bone attached by a ball–and–socket joint to the shoulder. The "lower arm" has two bones like man's. The end structure is analogous to the hand. There is a wrist joint and the primitive bone structure of a thumb and two fingers.

The shoulder blades are imbedded in the muscles of the bird's back. The collar bone (what we call the wishbone) merges in front of the breastbone, forming a V. A bony cartilage system which zoologists call the coracoids braces the shoulder against the breastbone.

While the bones are light, the muscles that power the wings are incredibly strong. For a man to be able to fly like a bird, he would have to have wings each about 70 feet long and the strength to beat them in the air about 500 times a minute.

**Feathers**

Although it is hard to believe, feathers are akin to fish scales, and are made up of pretty much the same protinaceous material, which is known as keratin. The beak and claws consist of the same fibrous tissue. Developing from follicles in the skin, feathers grow only in certain areas, but from there they spread out to cover all the bare parts. Feathers are really a marvelous invention. Light but strong, they insulate a bird from heat and cold, help protect him from his enemies, shield him from rain and sun and beautify him.

There are several types of feathers. *Down* forms the plumage of the nestlings. Then there are hairlike feathers with a tufted end, known as *filoplumes*. These are, with most species, concealed by the *contour* feathers, and help to insulate the bird. Contour feathers give the bird its streamlined shape, and provide the basic coloration. *Quill* feathers grow in the wings and tail; these are, of course, necessary to flight.

A quill feather is the easiest to examine. The central axis (although it is a little off-center) is known as the rachis (pronounced ray-kiss). The lower, hollow part of the rachis is known as the calamus or quill. At its base is an opening through which the growing feather is nourished. From the rachis, the feather fans out in a flat vane that is wider on one side than the other. The rays are known as barbs. Each of these is like another tiny feather, and they are laced together by interlocking hooks. Sometimes a feather is "split" and these tiny hooks come apart, but the bird can lock them again by preening and shaking his feathers.

Removed from the indoor flight where he was on hard seed and placed in a breeding aviary where the pairs were being fed soaked oats and green food, this cock was suffering from acute bowel inflammation in three days due to the change in diet.

HARRY LACEY

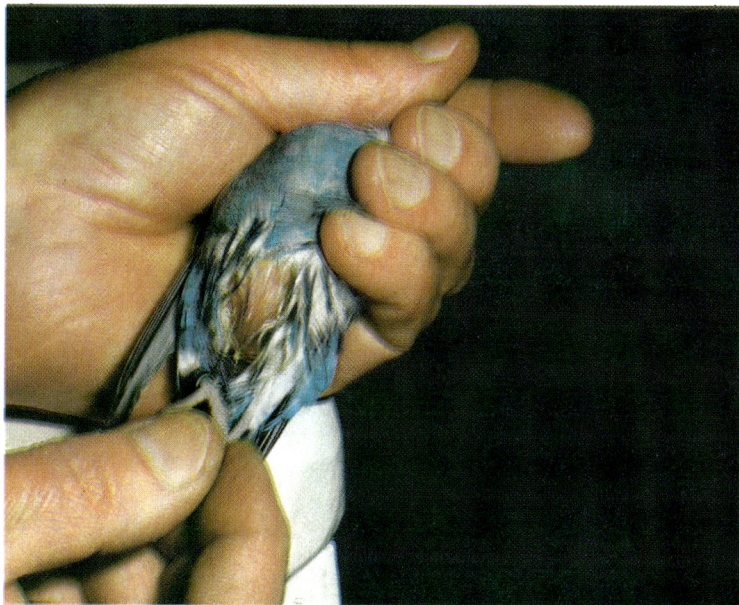

At the base of the tail, there is an oil gland. The parakeet uses its beak to spread oil from this gland into its feathers to make them waterproof.

## Molting

Feathers are shed at least once a year, and sometimes more often under indoor conditions. The molt is controlled to some degree by the change of daylight hours, by temperature, humidity, nutrition, egg-laying, etc. Normally, the spring molt begins in late February and continues into the middle

This keet is suffering from French Molt as well as diarrhea and over-grown or jutting beak.

of April. The autumn molt begins in August. Each takes about six weeks. However, with the artificial light and unnatural temperature of our homes, a budgie may molt all year round, or at any time during the year.

The first, or so-called "baby" molt takes place when the bird is about three months old, no matter what the time of the year. This is when he loses the baby stripes on his forehead, and the dark spots around the throat appear. At first glance, each spot seems to be formed by several feathers, but close examination will reveal it is a single feather.

New feathers soon grow from the follicles of the old ones. It is wise to pull out a badly broken feather, in order to give the new one a chance to start growing immediately. Otherwise, you must wait until the stump is molted. Since having a feather pulled is momentarily painful, hold the feather's base firmly and give one quick jerk. Remember that a parakeet's feathers, particularly those in the tail, are loosely attached to his body for defense. An enemy seizing him is often left with just a mouthful of feathers, while the intended victim flies off unharmed.

Some parakeets, when bored, have a tendency to pluck their own (or a cagemate's) feathers, much as nervous people bite their fingernails. This bad habit is discussed more fully in the chapter on Health.

At no time should a normal molt leave the bird with bare spots, nor should he lose the ability to fly at any time during the molt. (See page 217.)

## Beak

The most outstanding feature of budgerigars is the beak, which is hooked like those of the birds of prey although the parakeet is not carnivorous. The upper mandible of raptores is fixed to the skull, while the same structure in the parakeet is hinged and movable. Beaks are controlled by extremely strong muscles. It is not unusual for some budgies to gnaw through wood.

Since both the upper and lower mandibles are movable, the birds get a tremendous purchase when biting. They also use their beaks to help them climb.

Beaks are made of the same hornlike material (keratin) as the claws and feathers, and continue growing throughout the bird's life. In the wild, they are kept worn down by the constant search for food. In captivity, they must, in some cases, be trimmed.

## Smell

This is a moot question, but observation has led me to the conclusion that parakeets have little or no real sense of smell. It was once thought that birds of prey and carrion eaters must have a strong sense of smell to guide them to their food, but experiments to prove this have never been conclusive. It is most probably their acute eyesight that guides them to their food.

The nostrils are situated just above the top of the beak, and are surrounded by a small area devoid of feathers known as the cere. This is a distinctive feature that helps us differentiate the sexes.

While their sense of smell is probably inferior to a human's, parakeets are much more susceptible to gas in the air. A gas leak which might cause only minor discomfort to a human could kill a bird.

## Taste

Like the sense of smell, the sense of taste is not well developed. We must remember that birds bolt their food whole, without chewing, so there is little need for taste in the sense that we know it. I have found that parakeets undoubtedly taste strong spices and kindred flavors in their food. On the other hand, one experimenter tells of feeding a budgie bits of bread dipped in quinine, with the bird apparently relishing the bitter taste—perhaps because most seeds are bitter. Ornithologists tell us that the birds do have taste buds, but these are situated at the back of the mouth. I am of the opinion that budgies recognize sweetness, and like it. I think birds select their food more by sight and instinct than by taste. It is often difficult to change a bird from one seed to another, and sometimes it can be done only by intermingling the new seed with the old and gradually eliminating the old. Parakeets seem to like salt; at least this is the only way I can account for the way some parakeets love to lick their owners' skin.

Not too much research has been done on the sense of taste in birds, but enough has been done to know that of all birds, parakeets probably have the most sensitive sense of taste. Perhaps some of my readers would like to experiment and report.

## Tongue

The parakeet's tongue is thick, blunt and remarkably sensitive to touch.

At one time it was thought that parakeets used their tongues when imitating the human voice. We know that this is not true, and that the tongue is only a poor help, if any, when it comes to speaking. The sounds are formed in the throat.

Until quite recent times, talking birds were mutilated by having their tongues split to make them loose, because it was thought that this enhanced their ability to talk. Such mutilation is, of course, quite useless, and I am happy to report that this vicious practice has virtually died out. How it started I'll never know, because it accomplishes nothing.

## Hearing

The parakeets, in common with all birds, have their ear apertures concealed by feathers. Because of this, many persons mistakenly believe that birds have no ears. This is far from true—they have a highly acute sense of hearing. If this were not so, how would they learn to mimic sounds so well? It is surprising over what a great distance parakeets can hear other birds calling, and how quickly they react when hearing their owner's voice.

## Vision

The eyes seem to be constructed somewhat on the principle of a telescope, adapting them to long distance vision. They

A color mosaic hen, a form of bicolor. The type is poor but the colors are charming. The nails need to be clipped, otherwise she may puncture her eggs.

are situated centrally; the birds can see backwards and forwards and up and down; also, each eye can be focused independently. Intensity of light causes the pupil to dilate or contract. When the bird is excited or overcome with ardor, the pupil will expand and contract rapidly. This is perfectly normal. Parakeets move about mainly during the daylight hours, and do not like to move in the dark.

Because of the eye placement, it is possible for parakeets to see on both sides at the same time, but they cannot focus both eyes on one subject unless it is immediately in front of them. Birds can distinguish different colors, and they can also see the range of shades from black to white. Birds can be frightened by brightly colored fabrics when they are moved suddenly.

## Eyelids

Parakeets have three eyelids: an upper, a lower, and a semi-transparent membranous one called a nictating membrane. This can be drawn horizontally across between the eyeball and the outer lids, and is involved in cleansing, lubricating and protecting the eye.

The upper and lower (which is larger) lids have lashes. These are not hairs, but short, barbless feathers.

## Digestion

Food is swallowed whole. It passes down the long esophagus into the crop, which is just beyond the base of the neck, and here it is stored and moistened. When the crop is full, it can often be seen protruding at the front of or toward one side of the breast. The crop enables the parakeet to eat a large amount of food, to save it and digest it later or regurgitate it to feed its young.

From the crop, food passes by peristaltic (wavelike) movements slowly into the first part of the stomach, known as the proventriculus. Here gastric juice is secreted. The food then passes into a second part of the stomach, the gizzard. This is a tough-walled organ in which the food is ground with grit and pebbles that the bird has swallowed. As we know, birds have no teeth, so the gizzard acts like a grist mill to crush their food. From the gizzard the food, now in a semi-fluid state, passes into the first part of the small intestine where the liver and pancreas contribute their necessary secretions, and from which the nutrients are assimilated into the system. The waste matter passes into the large intestine, and from there into a chamber, the cloaca, from which it is discharged through the anus, or as it is more commonly called in birds, the vent.

Urine from the kidneys also passes into the cloaca, and is excreted with the solid masses. Birds do not have a separate external urinary organ, nor is the urine of a healthy bird liquid; it is semi-solid.

## Sex Organs

The body cavity also contains the sex organs, which in the case of the male consist of a pair of testes from which tiny tubes carry sperm to the cloaca. In the act of mating, the male bird mounts the female and presses the lips of his cloaca against hers, ejaculating his sperm.

The female organs consist of an ovary and oviduct. The embryonic female develops two ovaries, but the right one and its duct quickly degenerate, so to all intents and purposes she has only one ovary and one oviduct—the left. Situated near the kidneys at the back of the body cavity, the ovary resembles a tiny bunch of grapes.

## Egg Laying

Enclosed in the ovary are thousands—some say millions—of ova or egg cells; these are also known as oöcytes. These cells develop while the embryo is still in the egg and are all there —enough to last several lifetimes—when the chick is born. These oöcytes, with the addition of vitellin, nucleoprotein and other proteins, lecithin and cholesterol make up the yellow yolk matter. Later on, albumin (the white), the shell membrane and the shell itself are added to form the egg— fertile or infertile as the case may be. The protein of the albumin and the oils of the yolk are there to nourish the embryo if it should develop.

When an ovum with its bed of yolk is ripe, it breaks away and is drawn into the funnel-like mouth of the oviduct, or egg passage. There it may, or may not, encounter the male

Three nice Pied cocks; two Yellow and Green, the third Gray and White. All three have the same show fault—missing throat spots and broken ▶ cheek patches.

sperm which, after mating, have "swum" up into the neck of the oviduct. If it does encounter the male sperm, the ovum is fertilized and will, if all goes well, develop into a bird.

It is at this point that the genetic heritage of the bird is established—with male and female each contributing half of the genes.

The egg, fertilized or not, now travels down the oviduct, dividing into two, then four, then eight, and so on (in geometric progression), cells, and as it travels it collects swirls of albumin, secreted by the glands in the oviduct. Finally, two enclosing membranes form around the albumin, and around these, shortly before the egg is laid, other glands deposit calcareous matter to form the shell.

Numerous facts can affect the deposition of calcium on the shell. Among these are nutrition (amount of calcium, phosphorus, manganese and vitamin D ingested by the hen), season, age of hen and environmental temperature. For instance, high temperature decreases the amount of calcium deposited on the egg. Hypothermia (low body temperature) causes premature egg expulsion, and prevents calcium deposition, resulting in soft-shelled eggs.

Once the shell is hardened, the egg is ready to be laid, its blunt end forward and pointed end back. The walls of the oviduct are equipped with constrictor muscles which exert pressure around the pointed end, pushing it forward, much as wet soap skids out of your hand when you squeeze it. This pressure continues until the egg is laid. But sometimes pressure occurs not only behind the egg, but in front of it, and sometimes the egg is soft-shelled, whereupon its yielding surface merely absorbs the constricting pressure. In either case, egg binding will occur, and the mother will have to be assisted (see Egg Binding in my chapter on Health).

The egg is then laid, passing into the cloaca and out through the vent. It may or may not be fertile. A female parakeet, like a hen, may lay eggs even if she has not been impregnated, but an embryo can develop only if she has been. The whole journey takes 48 hours.

Development of the embryo can occur only if the eggs are kept warm, and this the parent birds (usually the mother), do by sitting on them during incubation.

HARRY LACEY

Budgies and dogs can not only coexist amicably, they can become good friends; but they must be introduced properly and taught to respect each other.

# XV   Health Care

When parakeets are well fed and housed under sanitary conditions, free from dampness and drafts, they suffer very few ailments. However, certain unforeseen instances may occur, and a bird become sick. One of the first indications that a bird is not feeling well is his general listlessness, with his feathers fluffed out and possibly his head tucked into his back feathers. Constantly tucking up one foot, or closing one or both eyes, are also warning signals. Whenever a bird is in this condition, it behooves the owner to examine him carefully to see if the eyes are dull, and whether or not the droppings are watery or off-colored (see page 204). More dangerous warning signs are the loss of appetite or an obviously increased appetite, particularly for water, a rapid rise in the respiratory rate, emaciation, weakness and, obviously, coma.

The healthy parakeet sleeps with his head pulled back into his shoulders. But when he is ill, the head may droop drowsily farther and farther forward into his breast. This is almost a certain sign that something is wrong.

As I point out in my chapter on Anatomy, the large intestine at its lower end widens into a chamber known as the cloaca. This is the only exit from the body of all the body products—feces, urine, sperm and eggs. Since the urine mixes with the feces, the feces are never hard; however, in a healthy bird neither are they thin and mucousy.

Since a bird's digestive system is so different from ours, he must eat almost constantly. A parakeet can starve to death by going without food for 48 hours. This applies to sick birds as well. Never withhold food from a sick bird; on the contrary, tempt him to eat, offering all of his favorite foods. Many ailing birds have died not of what ailed them, but of starvation.

## Veterinary Treatment

Not every veterinarian is skilled in the practice of treating

Suggested construction of a hospital cage.

MICHAEL YOUENS

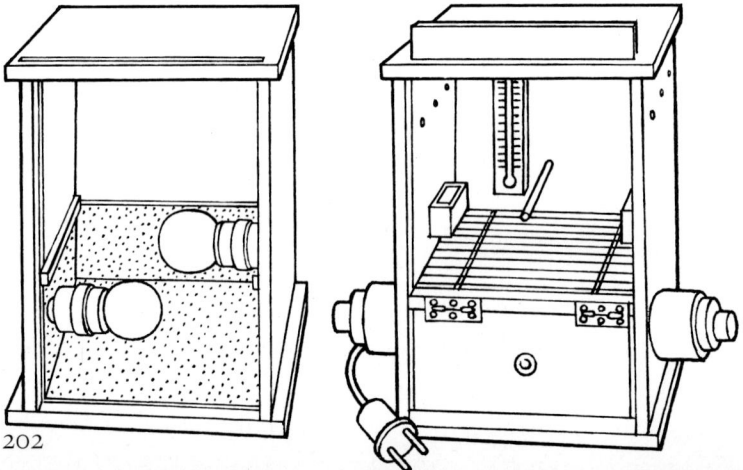

202

cage birds, and it would be wise to line up one in advance so you will know where to go when you are in need of professional services. The owner of your local pet shop will probably be able to recommend one in the neighborhood.

If it does become necessary to take your bird to the vet, carry him in his regular cage, if at all possible, and do *not* clean it first, because the first thing that the vet will want to do is examine the droppings. He will also want to examine the seed and everything else the bird has been eating, and will undoubtedly inquire about any sudden change in its behavior.

## Hospital Cage

If a bird becomes ill, the very first thing you must do is isolate it from all other birds in the home or aviary. Even if it is a lone pet, it is a good idea to move it to a different cage, so that its regular cage can be thoroughly disinfected. So-called "hospital cages" can be purchased or constructed, and whether you have several birds or an aviary full, such a cage is a wise investment. They are usually glass enclosed, and have a thermostatically controlled heating system.

If a hospital cage is not available, one can be improvised. Take a clean cage and remove all perches. Place seed and water cups on the bottom. Put a 40-watt light bulb next to the cage, and drape cage, bulb and all with a light blanket. Be sure that the blanket cannot touch the bulb and cause a fire. A "canopy" made of wire coathangers will help you drape it. Such an arrangement should keep the cage heated to a temperature of 85 to 90°F. However, check this with a thermometer, and if necessary use a lesser or higher wattage bulb to achieve the right average. The temperature must be maintained 24 hours a day until a complete cure is effected. Don't worry about the light keeping the bird awake; he can tuck his head under his wing if he wants to sleep.

## Aureomycin

A good broad spectrum cure is aureomycin, and even if you do not know what is ailing the bird, this is highly recommended, since it works well—according to the makers—on most of the respiratory diseases, infectious arthritis and bacterial enteritis (diarrhea).

It can be purchased in two forms at most pet shops: in tablet form to be dissolved in water, and as medicated seed to be fed exclusively for 15 days. Follow directions on the package. The tablets are usually dissolved in the regular drinking water. Normally, a budgie does not drink much, but the high temperature of the hospital cage will make him thirsty. If he is too weak to drink, the aureomycin can be administered into the beak with an eyedropper—four drops each hour for eight hours, 32 drops a day. For the bird who eats voluntarily, the seed is probably the better.

In the United Kingdom, antibiotics are available by prescription only, so you must contact your veterinary surgeon.

## Droppings

Since the novice cannot take a parakeet's pulse or temperature, or ask him how he feels, an excellent way to determine if there is anything wrong is to examine his droppings.

Anticipate this by examining the bird's droppings for color and consistency when he is in excellent health, and counting them. There should be about 40 every 24 hours, and they should consist of a firm black ring, with a soft pure white center. The black material is feces; the white urine.

The black part can be affected in color and consistency by the type of food consumed, but any change in the color of the pure white matter indicates an unhealthy condition. Remember, the healthy bird's urine will always be pure white.

Watery or mucousy droppings intermixed with white urine suggest diarrhea or enteritis, because such droppings are strongly acid and this will irritate the vent.

Yellowish-brown, puttylike droppings can indicate indigestion. Yellow can indicate an infectious disease, especially if it changes to green.

Bloody droppings can be a sign of diphtheria. If there is also a white bubblelike froth, suspect tapeworm.

The bird is fearless and the dog is a natural hunter. The two must be watched carefully whenever they are together until you are certain that no harm will ensue.

In pneumonia and coccidiosis, droppings are grayish white, thin and watery. In nephritis, they are gray and gummy.

It pays to note the condition of the droppings every day.

## Invalid Diet

The budgerigar should eat, even if he is ill, and everything possible should be done to encourage him to do so. If he absolutely refuses, and you want to try and save him, he will have to be force fed (See Hand Feeding). As I have already said, many birds die not from what ails them, but from starvation.

Since you cannot watch a bird 24 hours a day, the best way to determine if he is eating is to count the droppings; the average, as we have said, is 40 a day; if 30 or less are passed, the bird is not eating enough.

## Hand Feeding

As a last resort, if the bird is not eating, you must resort to hand feeding. Boil six ounces of milk, and while it is still warm, stir in two ounces of maple or pancake syrup. Beat in the yolk of an egg and a pinch of salt. If it is available, add 100 milligrams of an antibiotic, such as terramycin or aureomycin. This mixture may be refrigerated, with the quantity to be fed warmed to 80°F. before use. Feed this with a plastic eyedropper, a drop at a time. Wrap the bird in a small hand towel so he can't struggle, and insert the tip of the dropper in the side at the hinge of the upper and lower beak. Usually even a sick bird will grasp the tip when it is offered to him this way. Allow a drop at a time to trickle down his throat. Never squirt, as you may force liquid into his lungs. After a few drops, pause a few minutes for him to swallow.

Most parakeets ordinarily drink very little water. Therefore, when medication is to be administered, place a lamp alongside the cage to keep it at 85 to 90°F. This will cause the bird to drink more. (See Hospital Cage.)

Medication or vitamin supplements in small quantities may also be disguised by sprinkling them on a favorite treat. It is almost useless to sprinkle these on seed, because the husk is always discarded.

## Aspergillosis

This is caused by the inhalation of spores from various molds, the most common being *Aspergillosis fumigatus*. The spores can be airborne, or they can develop on moldy seed. Just a few kernels start the trouble. Sometimes seed stored in a damp room grows moldy in the bag or bin, or seeds dropped by the birds and not immediately eaten get moldy on the floor of the aviary. Moldy bread or crackers can also be a cause. The disease is not contagious; however, any number of birds can contract it from the same source.

The spores attack the lungs and air sacs, causing a cheeselike pus to accumulate. As the infection develops, the infected birds have difficulty breathing, lose their desire for food and steadily grow weaker. Some sick birds will stretch their necks and shake their bodies, as though trying to rid themselves of the blockage. Some veterinarians recommend potassium iodide in the drinking water (one grain per pint), but since it can have toxic side effects, it should only be given under veterinary supervision. Some of the broad spectrum antibiotics are also used, but their use should be limited, since other complications can ensue. To date, no really satisfactory treatment has been discovered. I would suggest, however, that any suspected case be reported to your veterinarian, as a new drug may have been developed since.

It behooves every bird owner to make sure that the seed he feeds is always fresh and clean and free from mold, that no seed is allowed to mold on the floor of the aviary, and that there is no chance of spores being blown into the aviary or cage from a nearby accumulation of wet hay or sawdust litter. Obviously, if the aviary does become infected, it will have to be cleaned and thoroughly disinfected. The sick birds will have to be destroyed, and the aviary or cage (before it is used again) sprayed with a copper sulphate solution.

## Asthma

As a general rule, this respiratory condition rarely affects parakeets housed in aviaries, and only occasionally indoor pets. The first symptoms of asthma are a wheezing noise made when breathing, and a general listlessness. If treatment is given immediately, there is a very good chance that the bird will recover completely. There are several inhalants on the market that should be used as directed. An electric vaporizer will be helpful. If it is considered that the attack has been brought about by an overheated room or aviary, the bird should be moved to fresher and cooler air. The sick bird should be fed its usual food, together with fresh fruit and green food and, of course, fresh water.

## Beaks, Misshapen

Sometimes birds are discovered with their beaks reversed; that is, the top mandible is tucked into the bottom mandible instead of the other way around; or sometimes the upper grows so long that the bird cannot pick up seed with the beak as it does normally, but eats from the side of the bill. As this part is not fit for this, it wears away, while the grow-

An untrimmed, undershot beak.

HARRY LACEY

ing tip—deprived of its normal wear—grows longer and longer. In other instances, the mandibles do not mesh at all, one growing sideways of the other. A misshapen beak will have to be clipped periodically, so that the bird can crack its seed in comfort.

The cause of these deformed beaks is sometimes genetic; at other times it is due to careless feeding by parents. When it is hereditary, neither the parents nor any of their offspring (even the normal ones), should be used again for breeding.

Careless feeding is discussed on page 128.

Trimming is not difficult if you use strong, straight manicure nippers. Be careful, however, to avoid cutting into live tissue. Hold the bird up to a strong light, so that you

How to cut an overgrown beak or overgrown nails.

MICHAEL YOUENS

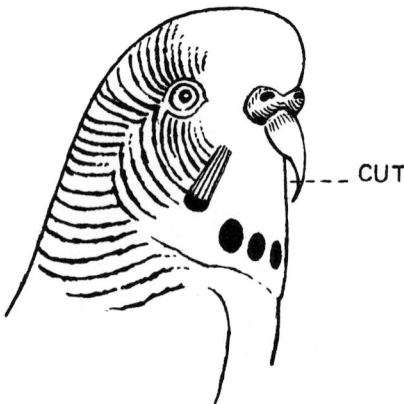

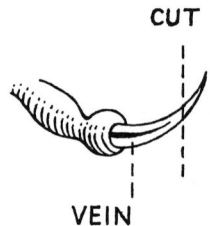

can see the dark blood vessels. Remove the chalky excess growth, cutting back to the live horny tissue, following the natural line of the bill. Use another budgie for a model or, if one is not available, a close-up photograph of a budgie's beak. If the beak is twisted out of shape, take the bird to the veterinarian.

## Bronchitis

Because the symptoms are so similar, bronchitis is discussed in the section on Respiratory Ailments.

## Claws, Overgrown

Claws (like fingernails) never stop growing. Overgrown claws are a menace. They keep the bird from grasping the perch properly, and if they are too long, they are liable to catch on something and be torn out. At breeding time, they can puncture the eggs. Claws can be easily clipped with small nippers or nail clippers. Cut just below the end of the small vein that runs partly through the center of each claw. Properly done, there should be no bleeding, but if there is, staunch the blood with a styptic pencil. If you are inexperienced, clip a little at a time, and keep examining the cut edge. When it changes texture, or shows a faint red, it's time to stop.

## Coccidiosis

Although coccidiosis is fairly well known to poultry raisers, it does not often affect the parakeets, particularly those in cages. Those in outdoor aviaries can contract the disease if they come into contact with wild birds, or even domestic poultry. It is usually introduced into an aviary by the contaminated droppings of starlings or sparrows dropping through the wirework. If this is seen happening, the owner should work quickly to correct the condition before the entire aviary becomes infected. Sick birds quickly lose weight, and a bloody diarrhea sets in. Except in later stages, infected birds do not become listless, nor do they lose their

The photographer advertised for birds to illustrate French Molt, Scaly Face and undershot beak. To his surprise, one bird arrived with *all* these troubles, as well as a claw missing. This is a good example of what a parakeet should not look like.

appetites. However, they do puff up and scurry around, looking like barnyard chicks. Fortunately, these days there are excellent antibiotics and antibacterials which can quickly bring coccidiosis under control. If this disease is even suspected, consult a veterinarian who will make a positive diagnosis by examining the droppings under a microscope and prescribe the right treatment. Here again I cannot emphasize too strongly the necessity to disinfect thoroughly the housing in which the birds contracted the disease.

Coccidia are protozoan parasites. The oöcytes, or spore forms, which are passed out in the droppings, are a source of infection. If the bird's quarters are not kept clean and food drops onto the floor, he can reinfect himself, thus increasing the severity of the infection.

## Colds

See Respiratory Ailments.

## Constipation

Constipation is more likely to affect caged birds, since they do not get enough exercise and may be fed too many rich dry foods. If a bird seems to have difficulty when voiding, examine its droppings. If they are very dry and hard, the bird's diet should be adjusted and a more liberal use of fruits and green food made. The first day or so, add a few crystals of Epsom salts to the drinking water to start the necessary bowel action. Poppy seed, mixed in with the regular seed mixture, is very good.

Once cured, there is no reason for a recurrence, provided the bird receives a proper proportion of fruits and greens in its daily diet. This is one of the reasons why human food should not be fed to a parakeet; sooner or later, it is sure to upset the bird's digestion.

An inability to defecate often results from excrement matting the vent feathers, preventing the passage of more feces. Pull out, or cut off these matted feathers after softening the mass with warm water.

## Coryza, Infectious

Because the symptoms are so similar, coryza is discussed in the section on Respiratory Ailments.

## Crop Binding

The crop is a small food storage chamber that holds food until the stomach is ready for it. Sometimes it becomes compacted with a solid mass of dry food, hair, string, paper and so on. You will notice a swelling in the esophagus. A few drops of oil should be given, allowed to set for about ten minutes, and then the crop should be gently kneaded with the fingers, forcing the mass up into the mouth. If this treatment fails, veterinary surgery is called for, but do not be alarmed—it is a "minor" operation.

## Crop Inflammation

If regurgitated froth (along with first a yellow, and then a green diarrhetic discharge) is seen, a serious condition is indicated, and unless it is treated immediately, the parakeet is quite likely to die. The preferred treatment is aureomycin or terramycin. A veterinarian is best equipped to handle this emergency.

## Cysts

These first appear as small pimple-like growths that gradually increase in size. While they are not actually painful, they do cause a certain amount of discomfort. If the bird is young and the cyst is on the wings, back or breast, it can be surgically removed by a veterinarian. I recommend surgical treatment, however, only for young birds, because the older ones cannot stand the shock of an operation too well. I treat older birds medically, painting the affected area once a week with tincture of iodine, and adding four drops of the tincture to the drinking water every fourth day. I have known this iodine treatment to arrest further growth of cysts and, in many cases, effect a complete cure. I must add, however, that it is imperative that treatment or surgery be given as soon as the first sign of a cyst is observed.

## Diarrhea

The voiding of liquid, evil smelling or strangely-colored droppings is a sign of diarrhea. It may or may not be the symptom of some other ailment. There are any number of things that can bring about this distressing condition—stale or fouled seed or other food, frosted or tainted fruits and moldy food, and contact with other birds suffering from a contagious disease. If a bird shows signs of diarrhea, even though slight, isolate him at once and keep him warm. If the vent feathers become fouled, they should be gently and carefully cleansed with warm water and a good germicide, and if necessary cut away with sharp scissors.

The patient should be given a few drops of Kaopectate, Pepto-Bismol or milk of bismuth from an eyedropper several times a day. Antibiotics are very effective, and they will usually cure a sick bird in short order with no bad after-effects. A dilute solution may be hand fed with a dropper, but some forms can also be offered in the drinking water, which should first be boiled and then allowed to cool. Since sick birds are usually dehydrated, they will drink enough of the solution to ease their condition. During treatment, the bird should be fed its usual seed mixture, but fruits and green foods should be withheld until the condition has completely disappeared.

**Dietary Deficiencies**

These are the direct cause of several ailments; they can also contribute to a general debility that invites other diseases. Rickets, soft beaks and the laying of soft-shelled eggs are caused by a lack of vitamin D and calcium. Slipped tendons may be due to a lack of magnesium. Eye inflammations and sterility indicate the need for more vitamin A. Iodine deficiency can cause goiter. Coprophagy (see page 75) is also a sign of diet deficiency. The answer is to evaluate the diet you are feeding, and supplement it with additional vitamins and minerals.

**Egg Binding**

This is the inability of the hen to pass the egg she is attempting to lay, a condition that is fairly common at the beginning of the breeding season. It has been my experience that more often than not it occurs with the third egg.

The cause can be a too-fat hen, a sudden chill just prior to

213

Steaming an egg-bound hen.

the laying of the egg, a malformation of the oviduct, a strain from laying the previous egg, a soft-shelled egg or an unusually large or misshapen one.

The breeder should not, of course, use an over-fat hen for breeding purposes, nor should he ever allow the hen to become chilled.

The first indication of egg binding is when the hen comes out of the nest box, and sits on the outside perch or on the floor of the breeding cage looking most unhappy, with her feathers fluffed out and the area around her vent swollen and inflamed. The first thing to do is, using an eyedropper, insert a few drops of warm olive oil into the vent. Then the bird should be immediately placed on the floor of a small cage and taken into an exceptionally warm room. The temperature should not be less than 85°F. Heat will do more than anything else to relieve the condition. Sometimes removing the tray and placing the cage over a towel-wrapped hotwater bottle, and allowing the bird to sit on that, will do the trick. Some breeders use an electric heating pad for the purpose.

If the heat treatment does not work, try steaming. Hold the hen's vent over very hot water, and try to ease the stiffened muscles. Great care must be taken not to scald the hen with overhot steam. Here again, before steaming the vent should be treated with olive oil.

After the egg has been passed—and it may take several steamings—the hen must be kept warm for some days before she is hardened off. A hospital cage comes in handy for this.

As a last resort, try to insert a pair of tweezers into the vent and break the egg. Pick out as much of the egg shell as possible, and chances are the hen will pass the rest. Be careful not to damage the delicate mucosal lining while doing this.

## Enteritis

There seem to be two forms of this deadly condition—one which is highly contagious, one which is not. The first is caused by bacteria, which can spread quickly if precautions are not taken at once. The second, a non-contagious form, is usually brought on by the bird's eating poisonous material, such as stale, fermented or moldy food or rotted fruit. In both cases the treatment is the same, and the owner must act quickly. The symptoms are fluffing of feathers, dullness of eyes and loose, slimy, green-tinted droppings, which in the advanced stage become blood stained. The treatment is like that outlined under Diarrhea, commencing with the complete disinfecting of everything that has come in contact with the sick bird. Here again I feel that the services of a veterinarian should be obtained to effect a quick and complete cure. Even suspected cases should be dealt with promptly, and if this were always done, far more birds would survive.

## Feather Plucking

Sometimes an adult bird will suddenly start to pluck his own feathers; this can be very annoying and, of course, disfiguring. Self plucking is usually caused by sheer boredom,

Trimming the nails. The budgerigar's head should be pushed downward so that its beak is pressed lightly into its chest. This will prevent it from biting or struggling.

or the lack of some mineral element in the diet. Give the bird some new playthings, or place his cage in another location. Be sure that he has cuttlebone or a mineral block. But if the habit goes too long unchecked, it is almost impossible to cure. If taken in the early stages, and a mixture of tincture of bitter aloes and olive oil is applied to the bare areas, the habit can usually be broken.

On rare occasions, a budgie will pull the feathers of his mates. Obviously, the first thing to do is to cage the offender by himself. Once a bird has started this unfortunate habit, I am afraid there is just no cure.

Another unfortunate form of feather plucking is when a parent bird—usually the hen—plucks the young. This seems to be a hereditary tendency, and therefore any hen who is guilty of it should be removed from the aviary and not bred again. It is usually the feathers on the back of the neck, the mantle and the soft underfeathers that are plucked— the tail and wings are left untouched. Various deterrents to put on the feathers of the baby birds have been suggested (like the aloes mixture mentioned above), but to my mind there is no cure, and a parent that plucks its young should be banished from the breeding quarters forever.

Some aviculturists believe that feather plucking is brought on by a deficiency of animal protein, and that feeding live worms and insects will end it. The mealworms sold in aquarium shops can be used for this purpose.

**Fits**

Because budgerigars are so highly excitable, they are liable to fits and seizures. These frequently occur at the beginning of the breeding season, or when the birds are molting. Cocks are much more prone to such seizures than hens. In most cases the fit is fatal; the bird will flutter to the floor and die almost instantly. When a dead bird is discovered, a good indication that it has had a fit is that the upper part of the beak is in the lower part, giving the appearance of being undershot. (If a bird dies from banging its head when flying, it may look as though it had died from a fit, but its beak will appear normal.)

In a mild case, a bird will flutter dazedly to the floor, and then fall over, kick its legs or flutter its wings. If this happens, isolate the bird in a small cage and keep it in a cool spot for two or three hours—with food and water, of course. When it has recovered, return it to its regular cage and keep it there alone for a week or so. A bird, once recovered from a fit, does not necessarily have another.

## French Molt

French Molt is a disease in which the flight and tail feathers of the very young birds break off or fall out. This usually happens just about the time the birds are ready to leave the nest and begin their first flights. The symptoms vary, depending upon the severity of the attack: in extreme cases, the body feathers are shed as well, leaving the bird virtually naked. In mild cases, only the two long tail feathers are lost— and they re-grow.

It is not a fatal disease, but it does disfigure the birds, rendering them useless; in the fancy, these birds are known as "runners" or "creepers" because they cannot fly.

The cause and cure, as this is being written, are still unknown. Although a great many theories have been advanced, no two authorities seem to agree. What they do agree on is that it is a very complex ailment which seems to strike without rhyme or reason; some chicks in the clutch get it, while others, with the same parentage and environmental conditions, do not.

Dr T. Geoffrey Taylor, who has done much research on the subject, lists the theories as follows:

a) a bacterial or viral infection;
b) a feather mite;
c) the Red Mite;
d) heredity;
e) a nutritional deficiency.

I personally subscribe to "d"—a hereditary fault which prevents the parents from passing on to their young the ability to utilize feather building essentials, or the young themselves being unable to absorb these materials. In my opinion, the only way to eradicate French Molt is to refrain from ever again breeding birds whose young suffer from it, or ever breeding the victims themselves. Chances are that a bird which recovers and appears normal never had French Molt in the first place, but had some other problem, as true French Molt is not curable. Such birds can, of course, be sold as pets, but they have no place in the breeding aviary.

Other breeders believe the cause to be nutritional deficiency, and that a well-balanced diet can reduce its severity; some believe it to be an endocrine imbalance.

Taylor has come to the conclusion that a vitamin imbalance predisposes the birds to the attack, too much vitamin A (perhaps the result of too much fish-liver oil) and a deficiency of vitamins E and K causing capillary hemorrhages. He is now investigating the possibility that French Molt is a viral infection that attacks the young birds once they are in this hemorrhaging condition.

## Going Light

This is not a specific ailment. It is a term used to describe a bird in general decline. When picked up, he seems to weigh less. If the cause of the ailment is not found and treated, the bird is quite likely to die.

## Mites and Lice

Birds can be attacked by Red Mites or Feather Lice under unsanitary conditions but, fortunately, there are ways of combating them.

Red Mites are tiny gray insects that do not live on birds but in tiny crevices of the perches and cages or aviaries, and often in nesting boxes. They usually come out at night and feast on the blood of the birds, and then return to their holes in the morning. They often look red because of the blood they've engorged. If you suspect their presence, throw a piece of white cloth over the cage and check it next morning for tiny red specks.

Feather Lice actually live among the feathers of the birds where they eat the flaked skin and feather oil, and gum their eggs to the shafts of the feathers.

This baby's beak is undershot, a condition which will get worse with neglect. It should be carefully trimmed as often as necessary with nail nippers or a file so that the underbeak will set in below the upper. If this is done, it will wear down naturally as the bird eats.

A skin mite attacks the bare areas at the base of the beak and around the eyes, causing the skin to appear rough and crumbly. Smear these areas lightly once a day with mineral oil, but avoid the nostrils. This will drown the parasites and the skin will regrow.

There are a number of commercial products available in pet shops to exterminate these pests. Ask your dealer to recommend one, and follow the directions on the package. The attack must always be made on two fronts—the bird himself and his living quarters.

There is on the market an excellent insecticide known as Vapona (a trademark of the Shell Oil Co.). It is sold in "no-pest" resin bars that can be hung close to the cage, or in birdrooms and shelters. Vapona exudes a noxious vapor, with little or no odor, which is death to mites and lice, as well as flying insects (fruit flies, for instance) which come within its range. However, recent reports indicate some possibility of danger in its use, so use caution.

Generally speaking, any cat flea powder, or the aerosol sprays designed for the eradication of such pests, are satisfactory for birds, but be sure the powder you use does *not* contain DDT.

## Nasal Discharge

A discharge from the nostrils that continues to reappear, or a cheesy deposit around the edges of the beak, may indicate a lack of vitamins in the diet and an all-purpose vitamin supplement should be added. While a nasal discharge may also result from a cold caused by a sudden chill or from being in a draft, a vitamin lack should also be suspected, particularly if the plumage is dull in color.

## Pneumonia

Because the symptoms are so similar, pneumonia is discussed in the section on Respiratory Ailments.

## Psittacosis (Ornithosis)

As with rabies and mad dogs, far too many people know about psittacosis only through hearsay. Although it is a contagious disease of birds and animals that is communicable to man, it is nothing to be unduly concerned about. It is rare, and today, with the broad spectrum antibiotics available, is curable.

Because the disease was first discovered in parrots, it was given the name of psittacosis, but before long it was found that other birds and fowls (especially turkeys) suffered from it as well, and its name was changed to ornithosis. No parrot or parakeet can be imported into the States until he has been held in quarantine for 45 days and treated with a suitable antibiotic under U.S. Government supervision. There is little danger of its affecting budgerigars raised in captivity, unless they come into contact with wild birds.

There is no easy way to diagnose psittacosis, as the symptoms are much like those of the other respiratory diseases (see opposite). It affects the lungs. Its earliest symptoms are a general fluffed-out appearance of all the feathers and a mucous discharge from mouth and nostrils, accompanied by acute diarrhea.

Obviously, if psittacosis is suspected, the assistance of a veterinarian should be enlisted immediately. He will most probably treat the bird with drugs.

Parakeets that have been immunized before purchase cannot be distinguished by their appearance. So, knowledgeable breeders treat their new accessions routinely with CTC-impregnated seeds soon after their arrival. This formula, known commercially as Keet-Life, is available in pet shops. It should be fed to the exclusion of all other food for from 15 to 30 consecutive days.

The symptoms of psittacosis in human beings are similar to those of lumbar pneumonia and, of course, should be treated by a physician. However, as one medical textbook puts it: "You stand a far greater chance of contracting tuberculosis, typhoid fever, pneumonia or hepatitis from your fellow humans than you do of contracting psittacosis from your pet."

## Regurgitation

New parakeet owners are sometimes surprised and worried when they see their pets regurgitating food. While this is not a pleasant sight, it is a sign that the bird is in fine, healthy condition. There is no way of preventing it, but it can be reduced by giving the bird plenty of exercise and a selection of toys to play with. I have also found twigs from fruit trees helpful; the bark is beneficial.

Frequently mirrors are the cause; the budgie thinks he sees another bird, and courts it by feeding it. Remove the mirror, and all is well.

Regurgitation may also be caused by enlarged thyroid glands caused by a deficiency of iodine. A few crystals of iodized salt in the drinking water should remedy this.

## Respiratory Ailments

The common respiratory ailments which sometimes infect budgerigars are bronchitis, pneumonia and infectious coryza, this last being akin to man's common cold.

The symptoms are much the same. The sufferer usually sits with feathers ruffled, sneezing regularly and looking disheartened. There may be a watery discharge from eyes and nose, and in the case of pneumonia, difficult breathing and a mucous discharge. In more serious cases, the droppings are yellow-green and watery, and the bird sits with his beak open and his eyes closed. Wheezing is a sign of bronchitis.

The patient should be placed immediately in another cage (or hospital cage) and taken into a room with warm but even temperature. Remove all perches from the cage, so that the bird is forced to sit on the bottom, and make sure there is water and seed beside him.

Mucous around the nostrils should be carefully cleansed away with a mild disinfectant and cotton-tip swab.

Unless the symptoms are so severe that veterinary care is mandatory, most respiratory ailments can be treated at home with aureomycin or with one of the other broad spectrum antibiotics, which may have to be prescribed by a veterinarian.

An electric vaporizer will give the invalid temporary relief.

Everything with which the sick bird has come into con-

These are extremely pretty birds but they all have serious show faults. The two on the left have multiple spots that spoil the look of the face area. To avoid producing birds with this multiple spotting, avoid mating two birds with the same fault. Smaller, clear, round, well placed spots are preferable. The bird on the right is undersize. HARRY LACEY

A severe case of Scaly Face.

tact (including toys) must be destroyed or disinfected, and his living quarters thoroughly fumigated before he is returned to them.

## Rheumatism

The older budgie is apt to develop stiffness in one or both legs and find it difficult to climb. This condition can be helped by massaging the legs daily with oil of iodine and adding four drops of tincture of iodine to the drinking water twice a week. Feed more green food. Always be sure that the perches are bone dry, and that they are not all of the same diameter.

## Scaly Face (Cnemidocoptic Mange)

This is caused by a small boring mite (*Cnemidocoptic pilae*), which attacks the horny part of the beak, the cere, sometimes the skin around the eyes, the feet and legs. (Until quite recently, it was thought to be caused by a fungus.)

It usually makes its first appearance at the sides of the beak. Small, whitish, crumblike growths develop there, gradually pushing out the feathers. These initial growths spread, as the bird scratches itself, to feet and legs, and sometimes the eye skin. It is not difficult to recognize, and fortunately it can be cured by applying one of the Scaly Face creams or ointments available in pet shops. It may take several appli-

223

cations before the condition clears up, and even longer for all traces to disappear. Even before treatment is started, it is important to disinfect wirework, perches, any nest boxes, seed and water cups with a good strong disinfectant like Dett or Lysol. Otherwise, the Scaly Face mites that are harbored there will reinfest the bird.

Daily treatment for about a week is sometimes enough to effect a cure.

Some breeders have reported that the Vapona bar discussed in the section on Mites and Lice is helpful.

## Sore Feet

For red, scaly feet, a good remedy is kerosene (in England, paraffin) mixed in a lanolin salve. Rub it carefully on the feet and legs for several days. The lanolin will soften the scales so they will fall off, and the kerosene will kill any scaly mites that may be present. Don't try to pull the scales off, as this will make them sore. They will come off as you use the salve.

## Stomach Trouble

There are a few ailments, commonly called "stomach complaints," which sometimes affect budgerigars, manifesting themselves as diarrhea and enteritis. These conditions can be brought about by dirty housing, stale or tainted food or too much green food, or the eating of toxic materials. Here again, first thoroughly disinfect all articles that have been in close proximity to the sick bird. Any fouling of the vent feathers should be carefully cleansed away with a cotton swab and tepid water.

There are several remedies that work well. Some of these are available in pet shops; others will have to be prescribed by a veterinarian. I, myself, use sulfamethazine (16% solution) which is given (in the drinking water) for three consecutive days, then three days are allowed to elapse and a further dose given on the seventh day. The dosage is four drops to a tablespoon of boiled water, or, if a large quantity is needed, a teaspoonful to one pint.

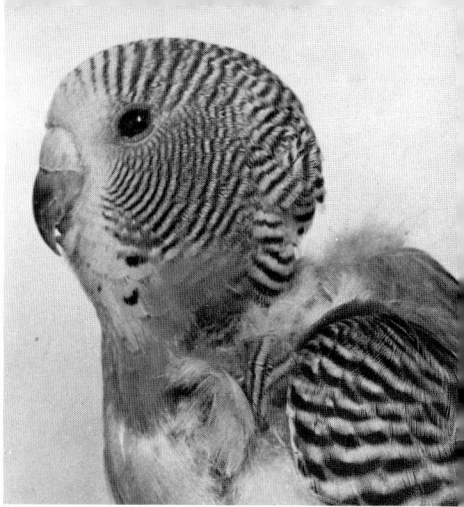

The result of feather plucking by an adult—usually the hen parent. These feathers will grow again.

HARRY LACEY

For mild indigestion, I use syrup of blackthorn, adding a few drops to the bird's drinking water for several days. This syrup is more easily obtained than some of the antibiotics.

During any illness, the bird should have its usual seed and millet, grit, and water that has first been boiled. All green food and fruit should first be withheld until the bird has recovered and its droppings return to normal.

## Tumorous Growths

Growths of a fatty nature that appear on the wing and chest areas are fairly simple to remove, but when they appear on the softer underparts, treatment becomes more difficult. In cases where surgery may be needed, call on a veterinarian for advice. Many of these soft growths can be cured. However, if the growth is internal, I am afraid there is no known cure at present, either by surgery or medication.

Overfed pets frequently develop fatty masses in the abdomen which resemble tumors. Cut out all fatty foods, including oats; feed more greens and remove the seed cups from 3.00 p.m. until the following morning. Follow this schedule until the lump has gone down. If this does not take place in two weeks, consult your veterinarian.

There seems to be an as yet not clearly understood relationship between tumors and excessive growth of beaks and nails. While they are not always connected, I am suspicious of birds which require frequent trimming. Much more often

225

than not, it will turn out that they are developing, or have developed, a tumor.

## Uropygial Gland

This is commonly known as the oil or preen gland. A large gland enclosed in a circlet of tiny feathers at the tail end of the vertebral column, it secretes an oily fluid which is expressed through two tiny ducts. The bird uses this secretion while preening its feathers.

The fat and wax act as a waterproofing material when spread on the feathers. Some zoologists believe that it also serves as a source of vitamin D. The ducts sometimes become plugged with hardened secretions, in which case they should be massaged with cotton and warm water. If this fails to open them, they must be cleared with the *eye* of a large needle, by putting the eye hole over the little nipple and pressing down firmly, but without undue force. The idea is to press the gummy substance (which can be seen and felt like a pea under the skin) out of the duct and up through the opening. Caution: Excessive pressure can rupture a duct and kill the bird.

The budgerigar show judge using his wand to move the entrants into position must always be careful not to startle the bird, as it might injure itself dashing about the cage.

# XVI   Safety First—and Always

Someone has written that budgies are accident-prone, and I cannot disagree. They do seem to become involved in all manner of unpredictable mishaps, but more often than not, it is their owner who is at fault, because he did not foresee the danger and take steps to prevent it.

Here's how some beloved pet budgies have met their fate:

Any number, playing on the floor, have been stepped on; others have been sat on.

One broke his leg in a clothesline pulley, another by catching his legband in a jagged wire.

One, exploring a refrigerator, was accidentally shut inside—and froze to death.

Untold numbers have been caught by pet cats.

One hung himself on the dangling cord of a venetian blind with which he had been playing. Another, housed in a cage with vertical bars, pushed his head between the bars where they were loose, then slipped down to where the bars were closer together and choked himself. A third lodged himself between a picture and a wall, and was dead when his owner finally found him; and a fourth strangled himself on a picture wire.

One, flying in the dark, dived against a wall and crashed behind a bookcase.

One, still a baby, flew full flight into an uncovered mirror and broke his neck.

One drowned in a toilet bowl whose cover had not been lowered.

Any number, perched on top of open doors, have been battered down when the doors slammed shut.

One was found jammed between a half-open window and the wire screen.

One nibbled the berries off a poisonous plant.

One died of poison from chewing on the leading of a stained glass window.

Another died of lead poisoning from devouring the bird shot in a shotgun shell.

One developed nicotine poisoning from chewing on cigarette butts.

One had his neck broken in a mouse trap.

One got sucked up into a vacuum cleaner.

One was gassed when, to keep him warm at night, his cage was placed on top of a kitchen stove pilot light.

One fell into a kettle of simmering soup. He lived, but in a state of nakedness for the rest of his life.

Another fell into a pitcher half full of ice water, and couldn't get out.

Well! you may say, how can anyone anticipate all those possibilities? And you are right—you can't. But what you can do is to never let your budgie out of his cage while you are away from home, and to check up on him regularly—as if he were a tiny baby—when you are. If you are working in the kitchen at the stove or sink, or using electrical appliances, realize the risk of having your budgie with you. Open flames, boiling pots, running hot water, electric mixers, toasters, fans, dishwashers, automatic washers and driers can all cause disaster. The heat generated by uncovered light bulbs can burn him, as can a cigarette held carelessly in your hand.

Mirrors and windows are always potential dangers, since budgies—until they become accustomed to their nature—often try to fly right through them. Once they've learned the nature of glass, they seldom make that mistake.

Since budgies are prone to strangle themselves on loose wires and dangling strings, it makes sense to avoid these, both in the cage and around the house. Never suspend toys in cages on strings, or wire cuttlebone or greens loosely to the side of the cage; nor should you spring the bars of a cage by forcing something between them.

**Fractures**

Occasionally, through some unfortunate occurrence, a leg or wing will be broken. This is more likely to happen to a bird housed in an aviary than it is to a pet budgie kept in the house. If at all possible, it is best to have broken limbs set correctly by a veterinarian who knows what he is doing.

Fractures require careful manipulation and splinting.

If the situation is such that no vet is immediately available, you must do it yourself:

*Wings*: A wing is easier to set than a leg. You will need an assistant to hold the bird. Fold the broken wing into its natural position, with the bone ends touching and the wing tips crossed. Use a six-inch length of half-inch wide adhesive. Wrap this partway around the body and *both* wings as they are held in place at the shoulder end, leaving one end of the tape hanging loose temporarily. Next, run a second strip of adhesive straight down the middle of the back, starting at the shoulder strip and reaching the wing tips, where it should be tucked under between the tips for about half an inch. The shoulder strip is then wound twice around the body, and over this back strip to hold it down. Last, fasten the wing tips together with a third strip of adhesive. This is important, because it helps the bird's balance. Leave the adhesive on for about two weeks, and then take it off gently, holding the wings firmly in place as you do so. To keep from getting the feathers stuck together, some veterinarians cut strips of paper the same width as the tape, but shorter, and attach them to the gummed side; only the ends are left exposed so that they will stick. Soften adhesives with ether, acetone or nail polish remover, but use caution as they can be dangerous to birds.

*Legs*: There are three bones in the leg: the femur, tibiotarsus and tarsometatarsus. Most fractures are of the last, the bone closest to the foot. In splinting a broken leg, the joints must not be included in the splint if at all possible. Such a "middle" break can be splinted by folding $\frac{3}{8}$-inch adhesive tape back and forth around the broken bone while it is held in place, giving a flat, rather than a round splint. Use a strip of tape about three inches long. Continue winding the adhesive back and forth, pressing it flat each time, until a thick pad about $\frac{3}{4}$-inch wide, with the fracture in the center, is formed. Press this together tightly to form stiff tabs on the front and back of the leg. This will give the splint strength. Leave it on for about three weeks.

If the fracture is so close to a joint that it must be included in the splint, splint both bones. This obviously will restrict the bird to some degree, but it cannot be helped, and if the job is done carefully, immobility can be kept to a minimum.

For this, a stiffer splint will be necessary. Purchase at a drug store a tube of Johnson's Duo Adhesive, or if that is not in stock, a tiny quantity of surgeon's cast plaster. The Duo Adhesive is easier to use. You will also need a few flat toothpicks, and a $\frac{3}{8}$-inch strip of gauze about four inches long.

Clip—but do not pull—any feathers that might get in the way of the cast. Have a helper hold the bird with the broken bone ends set together correctly. Apply a thick layer of the adhesive to the leg, let it dry sticky, press into it three half-lengths of flat toothpicks and over them paint more adhesive. Finally, wind a very narrow strip of gauze around the leg spiral-wise, imbedding it in the adhesive. Now, hold the bird's leg immobile until the whole thing sets and allow it to remain in the cast three weeks. Vanishing cream will help to dissolve the cast.

Much the same procedure is followed if plaster is used: building the wet plaster up in layers, adding the toothpicks and winding it in the gauze. Vinegar is better for dissolving plaster.

If the budgie nibbles at the cast, you will have to protect it with an Elizabethan Collar (see page 232). However, once the cast is firmly set, the bird should be encouraged to use the leg as much as possible to keep it from stiffening; for this reason, no perches should be removed from the cage, nor should the position of the feeding cups be altered, unless it is apparent that the bird won't move from the floor and is not feeding.

Since the patient will be despondent over his immobilized condition, pay him more than the usual amount of attention so that he will not pine away.

Never bind a broken leg with yarn or string, or use them to tie on splints, as the leg may swell and the string cut into it, cutting off circulation.

**Band Removal**

Should a closed band irritate the leg, it sometimes becomes necessary to remove it. This can be done with a small pair of suture scissors—the type doctors use to remove stitches without cutting the skin. The bird's foot should be held securely between the fingers to prevent breaking the leg. When the band is slit, do not let the sharp end slash the foot. It is better to cut the band in two places and let it fall off.

## Christmas Decorations

Be careful about letting your budgie play about the Christmas tree or among the ornaments. A number of owners have reported the deaths of birds from nibbling at holiday decorations. Whether it is the tree itself, the needles or some preservative material sprayed on them, plastic snow or broken tree ornaments, I do not know; but I do recommend caution.

## Drowning

If a "drowned" budgie is rescued in time, it can sometimes be revived by artificial respiration. I do not know of any cases where mouth-to-mouth resuscitation was used—although I surely think it is worth trying—but I have heard of an incident in which the rescued bird was held over a sink, head down to let the water drain out, its breast pressed gently inward and released rhythmically, as the bird was lowered and raised to create a movement of air. It took at least ten minutes before there was any sign of life, and another five before a heartbeat was felt. The artificial respiration was continued for another half hour, and then the bird was held cradled in warm hands for another hour before being placed in a warmed hospital cage.

## Electric Wires

Budgies love to chew on swinging electric wires—when they are live, whoof! a dead budgie. Not always. Sometimes they are just badly burned and frightened into a state of shock. I cannot repeat too often how foolish it is to give a budgie the run of the house without supervision. If he is left alone in a room where there are loose lamp or appliance wires, be sure to pull their plugs from the sockets.

## Elizabethan Collar

To keep an ailing budgie from picking at himself or his bandages, you can make a so-called "Elizabethan Collar." This can be made from a discarded playing card, as it is about the proper stiffness. Cut a circle $1\frac{1}{2}$ inches in diameter, then cut a $\frac{1}{2}$-inch hole in the center with a slit from the center to the outer edge. This is spread to insert the bird's head, and can be sealed with Scotch tape after the collar is encircling the bird's neck.

## Overheating

Never leave a parakeet in the hot sun. Indoors or out, the bird should always be able to move from pleasant sunshine into cool shade. These birds are quite susceptible to over-heating. Their feathers should always be "up tight," molded to the body. When they fluff them out, hold their wings away from their bodies, "pant" with open beaks and when pulsing is noted in the upper throat, be warned: the bird is on the verge of sunstroke. Move him quickly into cool shade—but not too quickly: not, for instance, into an air-cooled room.

The loose ends of the wire must be carefully stapled down so that the birds don't cut themselves, and the bars must be set so closely together that a budgie's head can't fit through. The litter on top should be cleaned, as it could become a hiding place for Red Mite.

HARRY LACEY

Fresh cool drinking water will help to reduce the bird's temperature.

## Poison

Emergency treatment is necessary. Give the bird a laxative! Four or five drops of milk of magnesia, given drop by drop with a medicine dropper, works well because it is alkaline and an antidote to several acid poisons. A few drops of hydrogen peroxide—dilute it half and half in water—is also good if you do not know what the poison is. If you do know the poison, administer a few drops of its prescribed antidote diluted in water. Many municipal Departments of Health have Poison Control Bureaus which you can phone for emergency information.

Paints, especially those containing lead or linseed oil, are a frequent cause of bird poisoning. So are mouse "knots," ant cups and the insecticides left on unwashed vegetables or sprayed on house plants.

Be sure no pills or other human medication are left uncovered for your inquisitive pet to nibble at.

After giving your pet first aid treatment, phone your vet, tell him what you think the poison is and follow his instructions.

## Spraying

Never leave a budgie in a room while it is being sprayed for mosquitoes, flies or roaches. Many beloved pets have been lost this way. Do not return your bird to a sprayed room until it has been aired thoroughly.

## Wounds

It is possible for parakeets to inflict nasty wounds upon one another if a serious quarrel takes place. It is also possible for the birds to cut themselves on jagged wire-ends, or while playing with something with which they have no business to be playing.

Clip the feathers away from around the wound (don't

pull them out, it's too painful) and wash it with warm water. Then douse with household peroxide and dust it with an antiseptic foot powder. Bad wounds will have to be sutured by a veterinarian, and deep wounds should be protected from infection with aureomycin in the drinking water.

Toes, due to the parakeets constant crawling and climbing, are particularly frequently involved in mishaps. It is not at all unusual for a keet to catch its toe in a crevice and lose the nail when yanking it loose. Unfortunately, nothing can be done to restore the nail, but on the other hand, loss of the nail doesn't seem to bother the keet too much. Treat as any other wound.

## Catching a Bird in the House

Enticing a pet budgerigar back into its cage sometimes presents a problem. Once having tasted freedom, they do not want to return to prison, and who can blame them?

Always leave the cage door open, and be sure that there is a "landing strip" at its entrance. If the bird won't return of his own free will, let him see you place a treat in the cage—something you know he enjoys: fresh greens, millet or a favorite toy, for instance. A toy bell, rung inside the cage, will sometimes pique his curiosity. Darkening the room so that he thinks it is bedtime may do it. If the budgie lights on your head or shoulder, but you have trouble catching him, try walking into a dark closet and then closing the door. It is often easier to catch a bird in the dark.

## Outdoor Escapes

When a tamed pet budgie escapes the house, he can leave a lot of unhappy people behind. I have often been called upon to help locate lost pets, and in many cases I have been successful. This is particularly true when the budgie was banded, and I suggest that everyone put plastic bands on his pets if he has not already done so.

In my opinion, pet budgies do not fly away from home intentionally. Through carelessness on the part of their owners, they find a cage door open, a house door or window open, or they ride outside on someone's shoulder or head—sometimes a dog's—and, startled by the wide open spaces, take off. Their primal instinct seems to be to fly fast and high, but once the first swift flight is over, they seek human companionship and settle down in areas where people are active, usually within a mile of their home.

The idea is to notify as many people as quickly as possible to be on the lookout for your bird. I'd start with the nearest school, or if it is Sunday, church; offer a substantial reward to the child who spots your bird and leads you to him.

I would also notify any nearby outdoor aviaries, as budgies tend to seek out other birds; also pet shops, neighbors (especially neighborhood children), the police (many people who find birds report them), animal shelters; and put an ad in the community newspaper.

A talking budgie should be taught to repeat his own last name and phone number. Many birds have been returned because of this accomplishment.

HARRY LACEY

Budgerigars are shown in standardized show cages.

Secretary John Rumble and Assistant Secretary Dave Carter are arranging the Class prize labels so that the stewards can collect them promptly. The winning birds are being marked before the show is opened and as the results come in from the judging benches the Assistant Secretary makes up the supplementary sheets which are inserted into the show catalogue. Time is limited, and there is a great deal to be done, so they must work swiftly and efficiently.

# XVII Exhibiting

To breed and to show one's own prize budgerigars can be a rewarding experience. How well I remember the first exhibit, many years ago, at which I showed budgerigars I had bred. When I was given the lowest possible award in a strong class, I was thrilled. Since that time I have won many top awards in almost all the big shows, but the thrill of that first win surpasses them all.

I am not going to devote any of my limited space to the various classes in the shows, as they vary greatly from country to country, state to state, and even budgerigar society to budgerigar society; or to the way in which you enter your birds in a show. I must assume that you will have visited a number of budgerigar shows before you decide to enter your own birds, and that you have come to know most, if not all, of "the ropes" through study and observation, both procedures and the prize-winning birds themselves. I have given the addresses of the leading budgerigar societies in the Introduction, and I suggest you write to the secretary of one of these organizations and ask for a schedule of shows in your area, and the requirements for entering.

## Standards

One of the first things the novice breeder must do, if he intends breeding high quality birds, is to familiarize himself with the official standards of perfection for exhibition budgerigars as published by these societies. Having studied the standards, visited shows and examined the winners, he will then be in an excellent position to know which of his birds are the most suitable for showing. At the end of this chapter I discuss the qualities of an exhibition budgerigar.

It goes without saying that birds cannot be taken straight from an aviary and sent to a bird show. It takes five or six weeks to prepare a bird properly.

## Show Time

While captive budgies will breed at any time of the year, the usual thing is to breed them in the spring, starting about March 1st; some anxious breeders set St Valentine's Day, February 14th, as the target date. This means that the budgies will be through nesting sometime in June—if they are allowed the standard two broods. They will then be separated by sexes, rested, reconditioned, the babies will go through their first molt, and, come late August or early September, be ready for showing. This is the beginning of the exhibition season, which continues until early February.

CAGE & AVIARY BIRDS

The author (on left) with his co-judges admires the bird selected as best budgerigar at the British National Exhibition.

Harry Bryan, one of the best known breeders in the world, judging a budgerigar class. Placing the whole class on the judging bench at once, he quickly relegates three or four cages to the rejected end. Then a little study and considerable shuffling enables him to put them in 1—2—3 order.

The scene at a British Open Bird Show.

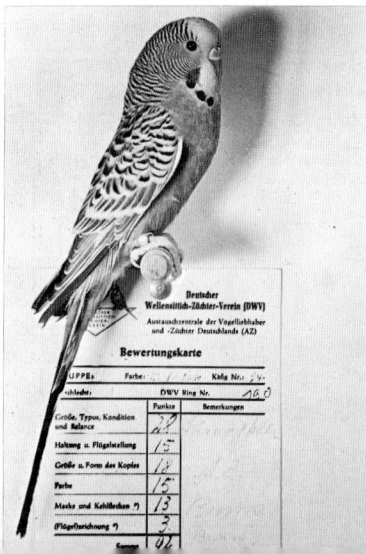

A German judging card and the bird that was judged. Standards vary from country to country. Judged by British standards this bird would have scored far below the 94 it was given here.

## Show Cages

Budgerigars are shown in standardized show cages, or at least they should be. This is to give every bird an equal amount of space and uniform equipment, so that one exhibitor does not "have it over the other." These cages can be purchased from pet supply stores, or you can build your own, following the official specifications of the budgerigar societies whose shows you intend to enter. They are usually 14 inches long, 12 inches high, $6\frac{1}{2}$ inches wide. They are white enamel inside; black enamel outside; the bars run from top to bottom. The cages and their equipment should shine like new.

This will be no problem for your first show, since you will be acquiring new equipment, but cages must be kept clean and in good condition for all subsequent shows. They should be cleaned carefully after each use, stored away in plastic bags, and re-enameled whenever they begin to show wear and tear. Check before reusing them to make sure there are no leaks in the drinkers, and that cage bars have not become so loosened or sprung that a bird can strangle himself or escape.

What about the floor of the cage? Some exhibitors use blotting paper, others sawdust. Most sprinkle the floor of the cage with a thick layer of the bird's seed mixture. Paper has its disadvantages in that the bird may tear at it, and have it in bits by the time the judge appears. Sawdust, when the bird flutters, will be fanned every which way into seed cups, water and onto the birds.

Water should not be kept in the cage while the bird is in transit; it will only slosh over everything. Fill the vessel after the cage has been set up in its final resting place. No harm will come since budgies can go several days without water with no ill effects.

## Show Cage Training

The first thing you must do once you have chosen the bird or birds you plan to exhibit is to train them to be happy in show cages. It is also wise to train a spare bird, or stand-in, for

If competition is not too keen, the faults in the spotting of this Opaline Yellow-face Cobalt hen may be overlooked by the judge, because he knows how difficult it is to breed a good Yellow-face in the Blue series.

HARRY LACEY

each bird you intend to enter since your first choice may, just as the day of the show draws near, lose a tail feather or a spot, or "go soft." This means that he is out of condition and should not be exhibited.

Some budgies never adjust to show cages while others do so quite readily. In fact, some young birds seem to inherit a show talent from their parents—if the parents are tame and fearless, the children are quite likely to be. Basically, what is inherited is tractability and a charming arrogance.

If, on the other hand, a potential show bird does not seem to adjust to an exhibition cage, it is better to return him to the flight. He may still make a sound breeder. It is pointless to show him if he is going to huddle on the floor of the cage, cling to the bars or keep his head tucked under the food cup. If a judge cannot see a bird from all angles, he cannot judge him and he will pass by what may very well be an excellent specimen. The bird's correct pose is on the perch, head up, with his tail at a 30° angle. He must also become used to standing quietly while being closely observed.

I start my cage training by hanging old show cages over the open front doors of my stock cages, so that the birds can go in and out freely. They are encouraged to use these show cages as much as possible by hanging their favorite green food or millet sprays inside them.

After a while the birds can be kept in individual show cages for, say, an hour at a time, gradually increasing the period until they have adjusted to living in these small cages for as much as a week. A good time to start is when young birds have completed their first molt—when they are $3\frac{1}{2}$ to 4 months old—since not until then will you know which are up to show standard.

Being caged by himself is the first thing a bird must get used to if he has been living in a flight with others of his sex. Settle him in his show cage early in the morning; this will give him the entire day to become adjusted. See that he has seed, water and the necessary appurtenances for all cage budgerigars. Then leave him alone until the next morning.

## Poise and Confidence

The next thing he must get used to is you and other people. He must stand poised and appear fearless when the cage is approached and handled, even by strangers. Go to his cage. Look at him close up at eye level. Talk to him; offer him a tidbit. The object is to gain his confidence. If you do not wear eyeglasses, put on eyeglasses. Get him used to them, because many judges wear glasses. Pass your hand slowly back and forth in front of his cage. Ask other members of your family to help you. Since he must get used to the passers-by at an exhibition, place his training cage in a spot where there is much activity.

Next, the bird must be trained to sit in the correct position on the perch. This is given in the Standard as "steady on the perch at an angle of 30° from the vertical, looking fearless and natural."

In Chapter VI, I tell how to train a parakeet with a Tee-stick. The same training should be given to exhibition birds. If a bird crouches on the floor, lift him back to his perch with the stick; use it to move him from one perch to another; use it to turn him around on the perch.

His favorite greens, or a millet spray hung high in the cage, will encourage him to hold his head up. Transparent poly-ethylene can be fastened to the inside of the cage front to discourage his clinging to the bars.

After they become at home in their show cages, budgies should be given some trial runs in their traveling boxes.

## Spraying

To tighten the feathers, about two weeks before the show start spraying the bird every morning with cold water. Be sure to do this in the morning, so that he will have the whole day to dry out. If it is a damp day, see that it is done in a warm room with a gentle heat source. Use an old cage, and sit it in the sink to do the spraying.

I believe in a great deal of spraying. It improves the appearance of a bird immensely. Spray lightly the first few days, then gradually increase the amount until the bird is getting really wet. Stop this daily spraying a few days before the show to enable the natural oils to reassert themselves. Never spray on the morning of the show, because birds must not be sent on a trip while wet. You will be surprised at the smooth, sleek finish this regular spraying produces. Some breeders use rainwater since it is so soft, but that is not always available; the next best thing is distilled water, or boiled water that has cooled. Do not be tempted to use mite sprays; even though they make the feathers shine, they can irritate the eyes.

## Conditioning

It can happen that one of your best birds will not be in condition for showing. If his tail feathers are bad, and you have time—two months—you can pluck them, and they will re-grow in time for the exhibition; this is true also of broken wing feathers. Spots will re-grow in three to four weeks. If the bird is overweight, cut down on his diet. See that he gets only his seed (no oats) and greens for a full month before the show; if he appears too thin, fatten him up by adding a high proportion of hulled oats (groats) to his diet. Be careful not to feed any foods that could soil the feathers unless you are prepared to bathe the bird, and a bath should never be given within a week of a show. For bathing, see Chapter III.

## Futurity Classes

Some shows have Futurity Classes. Birds are picked for this

event when they are only a week old. At this age, of course, no one can predict a prize-winning bird, or even a good bird. All you have to go by is the breeding. Special bands are issued for the Futurity Classes, and are placed on the nestlings that show promise; the prizes are awarded out of money collected for the bands. The birds bearing Futurity Bands can, of course, be entered in the regular classes as well, but only birds with Futurity Bands can be shown in Futurity Classes.

## Choosing an Exhibition Budgerigar

The chosen bird must, first of all, conform closely to the published Standard, since this is what the judges go by. A bird may very well be better than the Standard, but it still may not win. No bird is perfect, but the one with the fewest faults has the best chance. In selecting a bird, therefore, don't look for perfection. Look for imperfections and choose the bird with the fewest. He should be tightly feathered, with no claws missing. If he has broken or missing feathers, there must be time for these to grow back before the day of the show.

## Size

The ideal length is $8\frac{1}{2}$ inches. Most judges prefer a big bird to a small one, but what is more important here is that the bird, no matter what his size, be well proportioned. A fat bird should not be exhibited, nor should a too-thin or a weedy one. Avoid stumpy individuals, and birds with too-long tail feathers. There should be no suggestion of the "Long Flight" mutation in the exhibition budgerigar.

## Head and Neck

The head should be large and wide, with a good lift from the beak to the crown and a good deal of back skull. From the front, the head should broaden out to the shoulders. If it is too narrow, and too small in proportion to the body, the bird will not win a prize. It is better to have a bird whose head is too large in proportion to his body than one with a head too small.

The way the bird carries his head is important. Wrong head carriage can sometimes suggest a bump on the shoulder. The bird's tucking his beak into the top of the neck is good because it displays the rise of the frontal, causing the bird to look better than if he pushed his beak and head forward. If the bird carries his head correctly, a bump (if there is one) will be hidden.

Avoid a bird whose beak does not fit snugly into the front of his face.

The eye should not be placed too high up.

The neck should be short and wide; a narrow neck is bad. There should be three spots on each side, and they should be solid—not a series of pinheads. These are also known as the necklace. Do not show birds with an uneven number of spots.

## Back and Wings

Looking at the bird in profile, the back, from the crown of

Looking at the overall bird critically the head is good, but the bird is too chesty and the tail droops.

The chest of this budgerigar is too heavy. This results in too much weight above the perch, thus upsetting the balance of the body. A good diet and exercise would probably help. Stance should be natural, not require training.

the head downwards, should be free of angles. A bird that is too hollow in the back or too rounded (known as roach backed) should be avoided.

Avoid too any bird whose wings have scissor-like primaries that cross over at the rump. The tips should just meet or overlap very slightly.

## Tail

Low set tails, sometimes called cranked tails, carried at an angle to the body, can spoil the appearance.

## Color

The color and markings will, of course, vary according to the color variety of the budgerigar being shown, but in all exhibition specimens it should be clear and level and of an even shade.

## Stance

The bird should stand upright on the perch in an almost vertical attitude; he should never crouch. As he poses for the judge, the bird should give the appearance of a "haughty aristocrat." If he assumes any other position, he will be downgraded.

## Proportion

A bird may be right in all his points but if they do not blend together gracefully in the right proportions, he can be faulted.

## Personality

This is difficult to put into words. It is that indefinable something that makes a superstar out of an actor. Call it charm, an aura, charisma. It is the sum total of all the attributes previously described. It is what makes the difference between a good bird and a champion. "You either have it or you don't!"

## Entering Shows

Show people are friendly people, always ready to assist a novice and to care for the birds of such entrants as cannot attend the show in person. This is important, because, while most people prefer to carry their birds personally to and from the shows, and care for them while there, many others are not in a position to do this. A schedule of the show should be obtained weeks, and if possible months, before the actual show time. If the exhibitor cannot attend in person, the show schedule will tell him to whom the bird should be addressed. The proper party(ies) should be notified well in advance so that they can be prepared to attend to the birds and enter them properly. In return, the official(s) will send cage labels identifying the entry and class, as well as address labels, both for the journey to and from the show.

A list of Budgerigar Societies appears in the Introduction.

## Shipping

The birds will be in the exhibition cages, which are in turn packed in well ventilated travelling boxes with sufficient packing material to prevent the cage from rattling back and forth. In addition to the seed in the cup, loose seed should be placed on the floor of the cage where the bird can find it easily. Budgies don't drink much anyhow, and in any event, water would spill, so best empty the drinking cups.

The stewards of the show will see that the cages are unpacked, set in their proper position, fed and watered. They are also responsible for seeing that the birds are shipped back promptly and the owner notified of his success.

Of course, a record must be kept of all show wins.

Judging is done before the show is opened to the public so as to avoid any undue distraction while the judges do their work.

# Appendix

The "Standard of Perfection" for the Ideal Budgerigar as published by The American Budgerigar Society and The Budgerigar Society (England) are given below.

These are not the complete "Standards of Perfection." The complete "Standards," which are published by the various societies, include color description, show regulations and procedures, equipment, etc. and may be obtained by writing to one of the societies listed in the Introduction.

## Europe and America

On the continent of Europe, budgerigars are judged on the point system, while in the British Isles, and in America as well, judging is done by comparison only.

## The American Budgerigar Society, Inc.★

"Although our impression of the Ideal Budgerigar does not exactly correspond in every particular with that of our 'British cousins' overseas, our Official Standard of Perfection for Exhibition Budgerigars is very nearly identical, for the greater part, with the Standard of Perfection of The British Budgerigar Society. It was felt by the members of the Standards Committee . . . that there is need for some degree of conformity in the Standards if there is to be any uniformity in type and color classifications throughout our budgerigar fancy."

## THE AMERICAN BUDGERIGAR SOCIETY'S

Standard of Perfection for the Ideal Budgerigar

### TYPE

The following standard for type is applicable to all varieties of Budgerigars.

1. CONDITION
The term "Condition" applies to physical condition, health, cleanliness, full plumage, and training. Any bird not in proper condition may be eliminated.

2. HEAD
The head should be large, round, wide and symmetrical when viewed from any angle; curvature of the skull commencing at cere, to lift outward and upward, continuing over the top and to the base of head in one graceful sweep. Hens should have a lower dome, and greater breadth of head than cocks.

3. NECK
The head should be joined smoothly to the body by a neck of proportionate size. It should be short and wide when it is viewed from any angle.

4. BODY
The body should taper gracefully from nape of neck to tip of tail, with an approximately straight back line: The chest line should be nicely curved, and then taper gracefully back in an approximately straight line to tip of tail. The chest should not be unduly shallow, nor excessively full.

5. TAIL
The tail should be straight and tight with two long tail feathers, proportionate in length with size of body. It should form a natural continuation of the body lines, being held neither above, below, nor to one side of this line.

6. LEGS AND FEET
The legs should be straight and strong, supporting the bird standing, gripping the perch firmly with two front and two rear toes and claws.

7. WINGS
The wings should be approximately two-fifths the total length of bird, neatly shaped, well-braced, carried just above the cushion of tail, and not crossed.

8. EYES
To be bold and bright, and positioned well away from front, top and back skull.

★ Courtesy of The American Budgerigar Society, Inc.

9. BEAK
Neat, small and set well into face.

10. CERE
Neat and in proportion with beak.

11. POSITION AND TRAINING
Steady on the perch at an angle of 30° from the vertical, looking fearless and natural.

12. SIZE
The ideal Exhibition Budgerigar is neither too large nor too small, but rather an equally proportioned bird, 8½ in. in length.

13. COLOR
Color clear, distinct and of an even shade.

14. MASK & SPOTS
Mask to be clear, deep and wide, ornamented by four evenly spaced spots supported by two spots under the cheek patches. Size of spots in proportion to the make-up of the bird.

15. MARKINGS
Wavy markings on cheek, head, neck, back and wings to be neat, clear cut and well balanced.

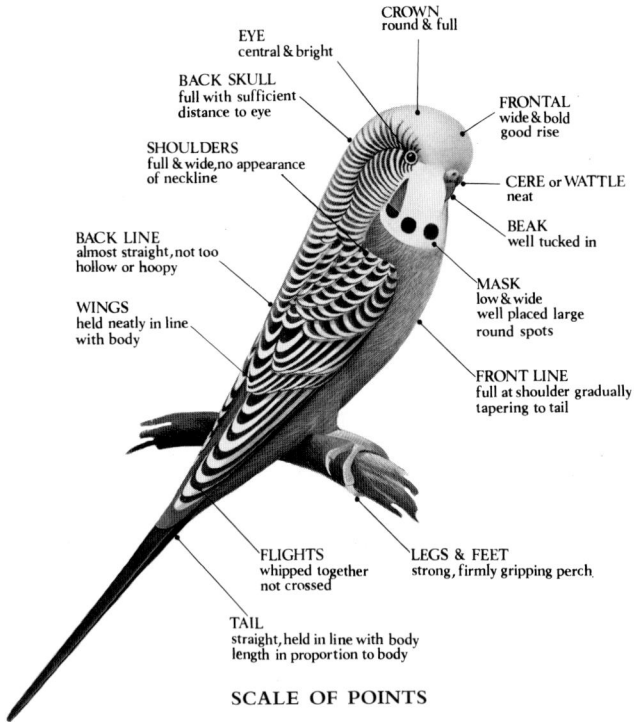

SCALE OF POINTS

| | |
|---|---|
| SIZE, SHAPE, CONDITION and BALANCE . . . . . 30 | Lt. Suffusion, Albino, Lutino . . 35 |
| DEPORTMENT and WING CARRIAGE . . . . . . 15 | Graywing and Cinnamon . . . 10 |
| SIZE and SHAPE OF HEAD . . 20 | MASK and SPOTS . . . . . 15 |
| COLOR . . . . . . . . 15 | Graywing, Cinnamon and Opaline. 10 |
| Light, Dark or Olive Yellow, White | WING MARKINGS . . . . . 5 |
| | Clearwing, Graywing and Cinnamon . . . . . . . . . 15 |

## THE BUDGERIGAR SOCIETY (ENGLAND)††

### The Budgerigar Society's new model

In the new ideal the committee, writes the Budgerigar Society secretary, C. D. Somerfield, has produced a bird standing at an angle of 30° from the vertical, with neatly fitting and well tucked-in beak, good forward rise and upward lift of skull sweeping over to an excellent back-line. The eye is well placed in the center of the head and there is a good deep mask with well rounded and evenly spaced spots set not too high on the mask. The markings fall back from the eye to give that greatly desired free-from-ticking look. Excellent width of face is clearly indicated as is thickness of neck. The breast-line is right, conveying just enough depth to give a proper balance overall. Nicely cut away between the legs, this bird stands just sufficiently high above the perch. The wings are cushioned neatly on the body giving an uninterrupted line from head to tip of tail.

### REVISED SCALE OF POINTS

| Type | Size, shape, balance and deportment | Size and shape of head | colour | Mask and spots | Wing markings |
|---|---|---|---|---|---|
| Green (Light, Dark or Olive) | 45 | 20 | 15 | 15 | 5 |
| Gray Green (Light, Medium or Dark) | 45 | 20 | 15 | 15 | 5 |
| Yellow (including Opaline Yellow but excluding Lutino) | 45 | 20 | 35 | — | — |
| Olive Yellow (including Cinnamon Olive Yellow) | 45 | 20 | 35 | — | — |
| Sky Blue, Cobalt, Mauve or Violet | 45 | 20 | 15 | 15 | 5 |
| Gray (Light, Medium or Dark) | 45 | 20 | 15 | 15 | 5 |
| White (light suffusion—including Opaline White but excluding Albino) | 45 | 20 | *35 | — | — |
| Whitewing (Sky Blue, Cobalt, Mauve, Violet or Gray) | 45 | 20 | *35 | — | — |
| Yellow-wing (Light, Dark, Olive or Gray Green) | 45 | 20 | *35 | — | — |
| Graywing (Light, Dark, Olive or Gray Green) | 45 | 20 | 10 | 10 | 15 |
| Graywing (Sky Blue, Cobalt, Mauve, Violet or Gray) | 45 | 20 | 10 | 10 | 15 |
| Cinnamon (Light, Dark, Olive or Gray Green) | 45 | 20 | 10 | 10 | 15 |
| Cinnamon (Sky Blue, Cobalt, Mauve, Violet or Gray) | 45 | 20 | 10 | 10 | 15 |
| Fallow (Light, Dark, Olive or Gray Green) | 45 | 20 | 15 | 15 | 5 |
| Fallow (Sky Blue, Cobalt, Mauve, Violet or Gray) | 45 | 20 | 15 | 15 | 5 |
| Lutino | 45 | 20 | 35 | — | — |
| Albino | 45 | 20 | 35 | — | — |
| Opaline (Light, Dark, Olive or Gray Green) | 40 | 20 | †25 | 10 | 5 |
| Opaline (Sky Blue, Cobalt, Mauve, Violet or Gray) | 40 | 20 | †25 | 10 | 5 |
| Opaline Cinnamon (Light, Dark, Olive or Gray Green) | 40 | 20 | †25 | 10 | 5 |
| Opaline Cinnamon (Sky Blue, Cobalt, Mauve, Violet or Gray) | 40 | 20 | †25 | 10 | 5 |
| Opaline Graywing (Light, Dark, Olive or Gray Green) | 40 | 20 | †25 | 10 | 5 |
| Opaline Graywing (Sky Blue, Cobalt, Mauve, Violet or Gray) | 40 | 20 | †25 | 10 | 5 |
| Yellow-face (all varieties in Blue series except Pieds) | 45 | 20 | 15 | 15 | 5 |
| Pied (Dominant varieties) | 45 | 20 | §15 | 10 | ‡10 |
| Pied (Clear-flighted varieties) | 45 | 20 | 10 | 10 | ¶15 |
| Pied (Recessive varieties) | 45 | 20 | ‡20 | — | ‡15 |
| Dark-eyed Clear varieties | 45 | 20 | 35 | — | — |
| Lacewings | 45 | 20 | 10 | 10 | 15 |

\* Points allocated for depth of colour and clearness of wings.
† Including clear mantle and neck (10 points).
‡ Including contrast in variegation.
¶ Including clear flights and tail.
§ Includes band.

Teams of six birds of any one colour or teams of four birds of any one colour.

Points: General quality 50
        Uniformity     50

†† Courtesy of The Budgerigar Society (England).

THE IDEAL BUDGERIGAR (ENGLAND)